W9-CAP-342

Multimedia Business Presentations: Customized Applications

David Heller

Dorothy Heller

McGraw Hill, Inc.

New York St Louis San Francisco Washington, D.C. Aukland Bogota
Caracas Lisbon London Madrid Mexico Milan
Montreal New Delhi Paris San Juan Singapore

NEW ENGLAND INSTITUTE
OF TECHNOLOGY
LEARNING RESOURCES CENTER

12/95

#32313802

Library of Congress Cataloging-in-Publication Data

Heller, David L.
    Multimedia business presentations : customized applications /
David Heller, Dorothy Heller.
       p.   cm.
    Includes index.
    ISBN 0-07-028080-0
    1. Multimedia systems in business presentations. 2. Business
presentations—Computer programs. I. Heller, Dorothy, 1946–
II. Title.
HF5718.22.H45   1995
006.6—dc20   95-8379
                                                    CIP

McGraw-Hill

A Division of The McGraw-Hill Companies

Copyright © 1996 by the McGraw-Hill Companies Inc. All rights
reserved. Printed in the United States of America. Except as permitted
under the United States Copyright Act of 1976, no part of this publica-
tion may be reproduced or distributed in any form or by any means, or
stored in a data base or retrieval system, without the prior written per-
mission of the publisher.

1 2 3 4 5 6 7 8 9 0   AGM/AGM 9 0 0 9 8 7 6 5

ISBN 0-07-028080-0

*The sponsoring editor for this book was Ron Powers, the editing super-
visor was Bernard Onken, and the production supervisor was Pamela
Pelton. It was set in Times Roman by David Heller.*

Printed and bound by Quebecor.

McGraw-Hill books are available at special quantity discounts to use
as premiums and sales promotions, or for use in corporate training programs. For more information, please write to the Director of Special
Sales, McGraw-Hill, Inc., 11 West 19th Street, New York, NY 10011. Or
contact your local bookstore.

Information contained in this work has been obtained by the
McGraw-Hill Companies Inc., ("McGraw-Hill") from sources
believed to be reliable. However, neither McGraw-Hill nor its
authors guarantee the accuracy or completeness of any information published herein, and neither McGraw-Hill nor its authors
shall be responsible for any errors, omissions, or damages aris-
ing out of use of this information. This work is published with
the understanding that McGraw-Hill and its authors are supply-
ing information but are not attempting to render engineering or
other professional services. If such services are required, the
assistance of an appropriate professional should be sought.

This book is printed on recycled, acid-free paper
containing a minimum of 50% recycled de-inked fiber.

Multimedia Business Presentations:
Customized Applications

LEARNING RESOURCES CTR/NEW ENGLAND TECH.
GEN   HF5718.22.H45 1996
Heller, Davi   Multimedia business presen

3 0147 0002 2056 9

HF 5718.22 .H45 1996

Heller, David L.

Multimedia business
  presentations

DATE DUE

DEMCO 38-297

NEW ENGLAND INSTITUTE
OF TECHNOLOGY
LEARNING RESOURCES CENTER

Other books in the McGraw-Hill Visual Technology Series

DataCAD for Architects and Designers by *Carol Buehrens*

Interactive Television: A Comprehensive Guide for Multimedia Technologists by *Winston William Hodge*

Lab VIEW Graphical Programming by *Craig W. Johnson*

The McGraw-Hill Multimedia Handbook by *Jessica Keyes*

The Virtual Reality Primer by *L. Casey Larijani*

CAD/CAM Handbook by *Carl Machover*

Multimedia Training: Developing Technology-Based Systems by *Angus Reynolds and Thomas Iwinski*

Contents

Chapter 3   Scripted Presentations

Chapter 4   Interactive Presentations

Chapter 5   Presentation

Chapter 6   Windows Multimedia

Chapter 7 Apple Multimedia

Chapter 8   Sound

Chapter 9   Video

Chapter 10   KODAK Photo CD

Dedication / Acknowledgements

This book is dedicated to

Shlomo Waser and Kevin Gardner

(Philips Semiconductors)

Who believed that we could do it and gave us the opportunity to prove it.

We would like to thank the following people and companies who worked with us and supported our efforts as we researched and wrote this book:

Bruce Roberts: Professional Indexing
Jolene Morrison: Editorial Assistance
Michael and Tanya Sukar: Technical Assistance

Adobe Systems: Rick Brown, Sonia Shaffer
Aldus: Chris Hall, Freda Cook
Apple Computers: Duncan Kennedy, Gabby Schindler
AST Computers: Holley Chronen, Michelle Monroe, Mary Reagan
Chisholm: Karen Horn, Alan Abott
Creative Labs: Beita Kenn, Steffanee White
DigiDesign: Toby Richards
Digital Soup: Mike Henkle
DreamLight Inc.: Michael Scaramozzino
Eastman Kodak Company: Carol Frieke, Terry McArdle
Gold Disk: Don Hellyer, Michaela Brehm
Macromedia: Douglas Wyrick, Jill Ryan, Mary Ann Walsh
Mediavision: Marnee Clement, Elizabeth Fairchild
Microsoft: Colin Hemingway, Lisa Prather, Shelly Wolmack, Tracy VanHoof
Midisoft Corp.: Chuck Robb
OSC: Josh Rosen
Otago University, New Zeland: Rodney Tamblyn (Audio Expert)
Regis Mckenna Public Relations (Apple Computers): Jenny Johnstone
Software Publishing Corp.: Lisa Spadoni
Turtle Beach Systems: Chris Buglia
Voyetra Technologies: Gigi Crisp

Copyrights and Trademarks

This section is provided to give credit to the copyright and trademark holders whose products are mentioned throughout this book. The authors apologize for any that have been inadvertently omitted from the list below. If any trademark is not properly identified, the omission is unintended. These companies hold trademarks and copyrights on associated products presented in this book:

Adobe Systems
Aldus
Apple Computers
AST Computer
Asymetrix
Chisholm
Creative Labs
DigiDesign
Digital Soup
DreamLight Inc.
Eastman Kodak Company
VideoFusion
Gold Disk
IBM
Macromedia
MediaVision
Microsoft Corp.
Midisoft Corp.
OSC
Orchid Technology
RasterOps
SuperMac Technology
Turtle Beach Systems
Voyetra Technologies

Delivering Your Message Through Multimedia!

Multi-ME- dia

You are on your way to taking advantage of multimedia, one of the most exciting new communication vehicles available today. This book empowers you to use the power of multimedia to present your ideas clearly, concisely, and quickly.

Herbert Marshall McLuhan, the 1960s media guru, said that "the medium is the message." He was talking about television and its impact on society. **We believe that *your* message is *the* message, and now is the time to use your personal computer and the wealth of multimedia presentation software to deliver your message loud and clear.**

Always remember that computers and software are just tools. They can't write effective presentation scripts, and they can't tell you how or when to use animation or music. They can't do the work for you; they can only make your job easier and provide a platform for effective presentations.

Your Message Is the Message

Modern multimedia tools are extremely powerful. They allow you to create action, import and create high-quality graphics and video, create and embed sophisticated sound that tracks animation, and produce dazzling special effects. This power can tempt you to use so much glitz that the medium overpowers your message, hiding it somewhere in the flash of special effects. Remember, <u>your</u> message is <u>the</u> message – in multimedia, the media are <u>not</u> the message. This book was written specifically to show you how to create effective presentations that don't get lost in the purple haze.

What Is Multimedia?

So, what is *multimedia*? Multimedia is an enabling technology that combines computer-generated graphic images with video and sound. What makes multimedia so special is its ability to empower people to participate interactively with the presentation. Multimedia is a computer-generated presentation that uses at least some motion or basic animation to add impact. You'll learn about both "basic" presentations and sophisticated presentations that incorporate animation, video, synchronized voice-overs, background sound, and sound effects to interact with your audience.

How to Use This Book

Getting Right to the Point

We organized *Multimedia Business Presentations* to enable you to quickly identify your needs, zero in on a presentation style that best meets these needs, and choose the right software and hardware tools to make your presentations a success.

Figure 1.1 shows how this organization looks in flow-diagram form.

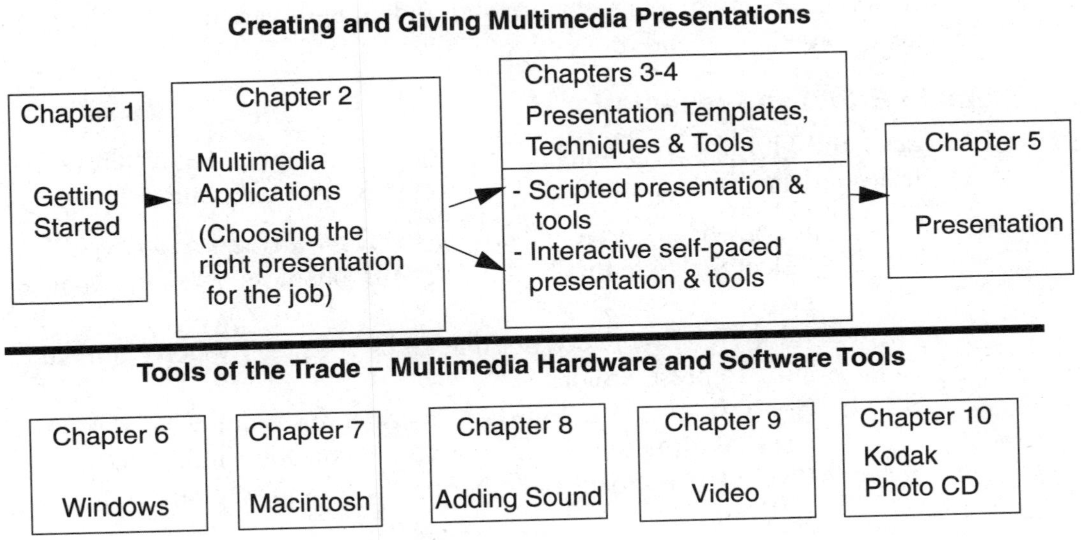

Creating and Giving Multimedia Presentations

| Chapter 1 — Getting Started | Chapter 2 — Multimedia Applications (Choosing the right presentation for the job) | Chapters 3-4 — Presentation Templates, Techniques & Tools — Scripted presentation & tools — Interactive self-paced presentation & tools | Chapter 5 — Presentation |

Tools of the Trade – Multimedia Hardware and Software Tools

| Chapter 6 — Windows | Chapter 7 — Macintosh | Chapter 8 — Adding Sound | Chapter 9 — Video | Chapter 10 — Kodak Photo CD |

Figure 1.1 Book organization and flow.

How to Create and Give Powerful Multimedia Presentations

Chapter 2 presents real-world multimedia applications so you can choose the presentation style that's just right for you. Chapters 3 and 4 show you how to create basic presentation types that you can tailor to meet your specific business or educational objectives. We include presentation samples that you can use as templates for your presentations, and preview authoring software for each presentation type. The presentation types covered in these chapters include:

- Scripted presentations
- Interactive self-paced presentations
- Continuous-run presentations

Chapter 5, *"Presentation,"* shows you how to prepare for and give effective seminars and one-on-one presentations. This chapter overviews traditional computerized presentation equipment and introduces the use of Kodak's Photo CD and a television set to give your presentation even extra portability.

Chapters 6 Through 10

These chapters introduce you to the multimedia capabilities of Windows and Macintosh operating systems, and introduce you to techniques and tools you can use when crafting your multimedia business presentations. You'll also learn about complementary audio and video hardware and software and Kodak Photo CD use and production.

Five Steps to Effective Presentations

We designed <u>Multimedia Business Presentations</u> so you can move around in it to meet your specific requirements. Just use these five easy steps:

1. Review Chapter 2, *"Choosing the Right Presentation Style."*
2. Select the style that best meets your business or educational goals.
3. Jump right to the chapter that takes you step by step from creation to presentation.
4. Go to Chaps. 6 through 10 to learn about Windows and Macintosh multimedia environments, advanced sound, video, Kodak CD options, and other hardware and software choices - in depth.
5. Review Chap. 5, *"Presentation,"* to prepare for and give your presentation.

Of course, you can also read through the chapters sequentially to get a good grounding on multimedia production and presentation.

Zeroing in On Your Presentation Scenario

Suppose your company sells a sophisticated product through VARs and distributors.

- You want these salespeople to have a basic understanding of your product's features and benefits.

- You want to show them how they can make money selling your product.

- You want them to devote a good percentage of their time selling your product.

You review Chap. 2 and decide that using a *scripted presentation* is the best way to implement your program. For this application you will send a computerized presentation on disk to your distributors, along with an accompanying script that allows the office manager or one of your "in-house" salespeople to make the presentation to all the people in the distributor's office. You skip right to Chap. 3, *"Scripted Presentations,"* and get down to work.

The creation and presentation chapters (Chaps. 3 and 4) include step by step techniques for scripting, producing, and distributing your presentation. Chapter 5, *"Presentation,"* shows you how to prepare for and give effective seminar and one-on-one presentations.

The final sections of Chaps. 3 and 4 include authoring tool software overviews you can use to implement your presentation, along with basic features and benefits of each package as it applies specifically to your application. Incorporating audio, video, and animation is also discussed.

You can turn to Chaps. 6 through 10 to learn how to incorporate audio, animation, and video into your presentation and to determine if Kodak Photo CD production and distribution are right for your job.

Do You Have an IBM PC or Compatible?

Back to the Basics: Your Basic System

For IBM PC or compatible computer multimedia production and presentation you will need a system based on the Windows operating system. Your hardware should include a soundboard, a video capture board, a video accelerator for crisp videos, a CD-ROM, at least a 250 MB hard disk (the more the merrier), and at least 4 MB of RAM.

At a minimum, your computer should have an INTEL 386 33-MHz processor or equivalent. A "486," Pentium, or later processor will result in faster performance and faster development times.

A Multimedia PC

The Multimedia PC Marketing Council, a subsidiary of the Software Publishers Association, publishes and maintains Multimedia PC (MPC) hardware and software standards and specifications.

Figure 1.2 MPC Logo.

The MPC mark (Fig. 1.2) means that the hardware or software is compatible with the minimum feature set and performance specifications required for multimedia computing. The standard includes an MPC-compliant CD-ROM drive and audio card, and is constantly being expanded and updated as technology moves forward.

If you don't already own a computer, you might consider buying a ready-to-go multimedia PC. IBM and virtually every other manufacturer of IBM PC and compatible computers offers a range of multimedia PC development and presentation platforms.

Figure 1.3 shows an AST Research, Inc., multimedia PC. This computer package includes a high-end 16-bit audio sound card, a video subsystem that delivers full-screen full-motion synchronized video, desktop speakers, a microphone, and a fast CD-ROM drive that is compatible with Kodak's Photo CD software. To round out the package, AST bundles a selection of multimedia software tools to get you up and running fast. Many computer manufacturers offer competitive multimedia packages and they are all reasonably priced.

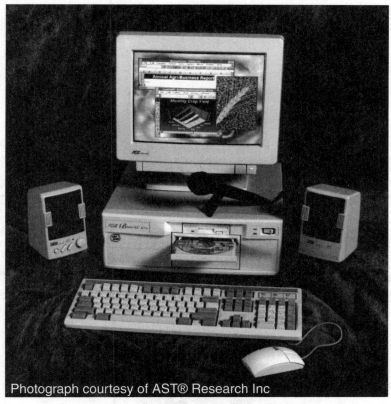
Photograph courtesy of AST® Research Inc

Figure 1.3 AST's Business Multimedia System.

Windows: Multimedia Development and Presentation

The Microsoft Windows environment with OLE (more on Object Linking and Embedding in Chapter 6) is an ideal and effective multimedia development and presentation platform. The proliferation of IBM PC and compatible computers ensure a broad audience for your presentations.

A wide variety of software to develop and make multimedia presentations is readily available for use in the Windows environment. To help you choose effective software for your project, this book includes detailed, in-depth analysis of some of the most popular Windows-compatible multimedia authoring and presentation packages, including:

- Action! (Macromedia)
- Animation Works Interactive (Gold Disk)
- Compel (Asymetrix)
- Freelance (Lotus)
- Multimedia Tool Book (Asymetrix)
- PowerPoint (Microsoft)

Each of these authoring/presentation software packages uses the power of Microsoft Windows to deliver presentations with different degrees of motion, sound, and user interaction.

Apple Macintosh Authoring and Presenting

The Macintosh: A World-Class Production and Presentation Platform

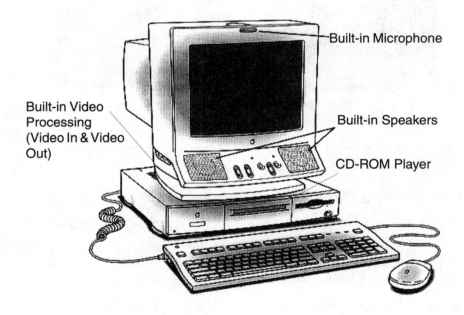

Figure 1.4 An Apple AV series computer and AV monitor specifically for multimedia production and presentation.

Apple's Macintosh Audio Visual Series of computers and displays (Fig. 1.4) include built-in audio capability, CD-ROM, built-in video capture, video edit, computer-to-television video capability and a built-in microphone. The AV computers feature high processing speeds to make your presentations smooth and crisp. These built-in features make the AV series computers world-class multimedia platforms. The latest Power Macintosh computers, with their superfast processors and ability to author and present in Windows or System 7 environments, bring a new generation of faster, smoother presentations to a wide audience.

Feature for feature, the AVs compete competitively with any INTEL-based computer. When you create a presentation on a Macintosh, you can play it on a Windows-equipped machine or port it, using special software, to UNIX-based workstations. In addition to Apple's AV computers, and the Power Macintosh series, Apple's series II Macintosh computers also make excellent multimedia platforms.

You'll learn about some of the most popular and powerful authoring and presentation tools, including:

- Action! (Gold Disk)
- Apple Media Tool (Apple Computers)
- Astound (Gold Disk)
- Director (Macromedia)
- PowerPoint (Microsoft)

A Sound Bonus

Sound is an extremely important part of the total presentation. As a special bonus, Chap. 8, "*Sound*," takes you on an in-depth tour of today's most sophisticated Macintosh and Windows-based digital sound editing and mixing products. We'll put you inside your own digital studio and show you the techniques and tools used by audio professionals (Fig 1.5). You'll learn how to use these sophisticated tools to add the impact of professional sound to your presentations.

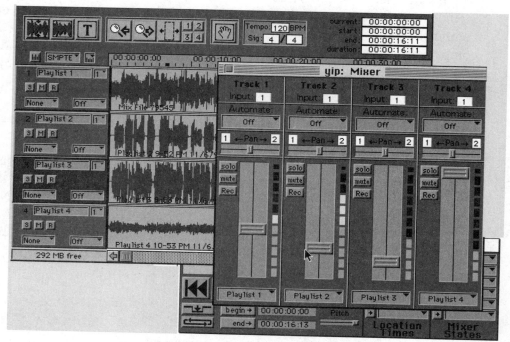

Figure 1.5 OSC's DECK II Digital Audio Workstation.

Video Brings It to Life

Digital movies, like digital sound, offer vistas of creativity that were never available before. This new technology allows you to create and edit high-quality digital movies and videotapes right on your computer. Chapter 10, *"Video,"* introduces you to digital movie-making techniques, including insight into special effects used by leading advertising agencies and Hollywood production studios.

The Adobe Premiere (Fig. 1.6) movie production package (used on both IBM PC and Macintosh computers) is reviewed in depth, and you'll also see what special effects can be added using VideoFusion special-effect software.

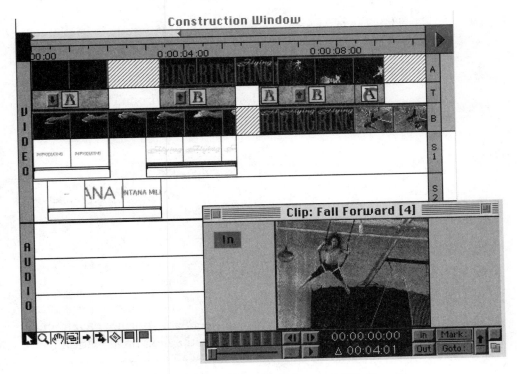

Figure 1.6 Adobe Premier's Video/Audio Workbench.

The Three P's

Helping you develop and give the best possible presentation is this book's goal. To get there, we've broken down the three most important steps, and willl cover each in detail throughout the book:

- **P**lanning

    - Ask questions and learn your material.

    - Outline or storyboard your presentation.

    - Write the script.

- **Production**
    - Use the appropriate tools of the trade to implement your script.
- **Presentation**
    - Prepare yourself and your environment.
    - Make the presentation.

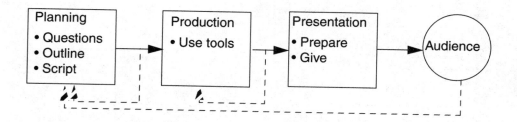

Feedback after each major step strengthens your presentation each time it's given. Get positive reinforcement and feedback during development, and incorporate audience feedback to strengthen the next presentation.

Your Road Map to Successful Presentations

Table 1.1 presents a brief book guide to help you chart your course.

TABLE 1.1 Road Map to Successful Presentation

Creating and giving multimedia presentations	Tools of the trade
Chapter 1: Getting Started	Chapter 6: Windows Multimedia
Chapter 2: Multimedia Applications	Chapter 7: Apple Multimedia
Chapter 3: Scripted Presentations	Chapter 8: Sound
Chapter4: Interactive Presentations	Chapter 9: Video
Chapter 5: Presentation	Chapter 10: Kodak Photo CD Basics

Choosing the Right Presentation for the Job

All you need to create and deliver your message is your PC and readily available and easy-to-use multimedia software, right? <u>Not</u>! The high-tech world of multimedia may be at your fingertips, but before you get immersed in its whiz-bang, high-tech possibilities you've got to carefully chart your course. If you don't, you may end up spinning your wheels buying the wrong software, using inappropriate equipment, and slapping together an ineffectual presentation. That's just what I did when I made my great leap from black-and-white overhead slide shows to computerized presentations, and it took me lots of trial and error before I got it right.

You don't have to burn rubber. This chapter will help you to laser-focus on the specific presentation type that makes the most sense for your job. Once you've decided on a presentation that gets <u>your</u> message across, just move on to the chapter that shows you how to craft it in detail.

Here's a short list of applications that are perfect candidates for multimedia presentations. We'll take a closer look at each of these candidates to enable you to select the presentation style that most closely fits your application:

- *Sales presentations* that save time and help close sales by enabling the salesperson to deliver complex messages clearly in the shortest time possible.

- *Marketing presentations* that give an overview of a product or products in the context of the company's strengths.

- *Training presentations*, including:

    - Seminar-style training presentations:

        Technical/educational, sales, competitive analysis, market position; training for students, in-house personnel, for customers and potential customers

    - Self-training presentations:

        Interactive multimedia that teaches the recipient about a product, a company, the market, about the competition - <u>anything</u>, including the software package in which the training material is embedded

- Training presentations for trainers:

  Presentations that teach teachers/trainers to give more effective presentations

- Corporate customer service aids, such as training disks with product information and focused tutorials that are sent in response to customer calls - all the information they need in an easy-to-digest form

- Corporate "big picture" presentations such as:

  - Financial presentations designed to get funding or highlight financial strengths

  - Human resource presentations that familiarize prospective employees with a company's structure, culture, or vision while highlighting employment benefits

Sales Presentations

Technology and innovation are moving so rapidly that it is becoming increasingly difficult, if not impossible, to remain current. As your products become more complex in concept and depth, effectively communicating their benefits and positioning them competitively becomes more and more challenging.

Ideally, you want your salespeople to go into a prospective account, quickly demonstrate the product's benefits, and qualify the prospect without wasting valuable time.

I work for a high-tech company that sells an extremely complex set of computer-aided engineering software tools to engineers who are designing today's state-of-the-art integrated circuits. Until recently, when a new software product was introduced, the salesperson would take a copy to the customer's facility, install it, cross his or her fingers, and pray that it worked the first time. Most times, the problem wasn't with the software, but with system environment incompatibilities. Wheew! Usually, after nerding around with the engineer for a few hours, the salesperson was ready to present the new product. But by this time the manager/decision maker had left.

Half the day was shot, and that was just the beginning. Because this type of software has so many options and great features, trying to give a short, focused presentation was often impossible. The engineers would invariably sidetrack the salesperson, asking to see every new gizmo, bell, and whistle, whether it applied to their work or not.

Once the show was over, often days later, the salesperson would often hear, "Thanks a lot for the demo. I'm not really sure if this is exactly the tool we need. I'll brief my boss and get back to you."

Granted, spending this much time with a customer is probably good for vendor - customer relations, but it sure isn't an effective way to qualify prospects, and it definitely was not an efficient use of our salespeople's time. We had to find a better way.

Multimedia to the Rescue!

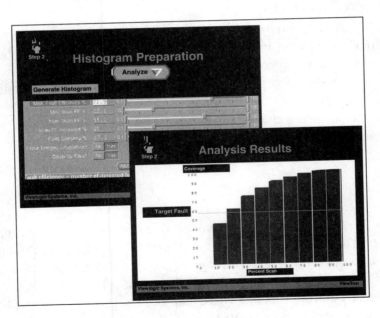

Figure 2.1 Simplifying the complex.

We created "simple" 20-minute scripted computerized presentations that visually walk prospects through our software's operation in a logical step-by-step way (Fig. 2.1). By simple, I mean that, although the presentation uses rudimentary animation to simulate the interaction between screen elements and the mouse arrow, it does not include synchronized audio, video, or complex animation.

Now, when we introduce a new product, we create a complementary scripted computerized *portable presentation*. The salesperson usually makes the presentation in the engineer's office on a portable computer or on the engineer's computer with his or her manager looking over the salesperson's shoulders. If we want to show the product to a larger audience, the salesperson typically brings a portable projection unit into a conference or training room.

Staggering Benefits

The benefits of this approach are staggering. We qualify our prospect in less than 30 minutes, and we educate his or her boss at the same time. If they're interested in our product they'll let us know immediately, and we can then follow up with a full-blown software installation demo. If not, we haven't wasted our valuable time, and that's key to maintaining good customer relations and efficiently utilizing our sales force.

Just Send It and Follow Up

Here's a way to prequalify your prospects without ever leaving your office. Produce *interactive presentations* that use hypertext and familiar button icons to make it easy for your prospect to get all the information he or she needs. Call to alert your prospect that the presentation is on its way, and ask that individual to plug it into the computer and review it. Then, simply call back after he or she has had a chance to absorb the material. This proven prequalification use of multimedia is time efficient and extremely cost effective.

Video Works Too

You can also prequalify your prospects by producing a self-running presentation, transferring it to videotape, sending it to them, and following up to check their interest level. The advantage of using videotape is that almost everyone has a VHS player. The only downside is that it is not interactive. However, in most cases this approach does a great job. You'll learn how to put your presentation on videotape in Chapter 5.

Close That Sale with Multimedia

No matter what product or service you are offering, you have to take your prospect through a few very well defined steps before you can close the sale. You <u>don't</u> have to be in a high-tech business to benefit from multimedia. You can be selling insurance, mutual funds, financial services, educational opportunities, diaper services, or jet aircraft.

1. First, you have to educate the prospect. He or she has to have confidence in your company and understand what your company's product or service does.
2. Next, you have to show how your product or service will benefit the prospect.
3. Finally, you have to answer questions, overcome objections, and close the sale.

A well-crafted multimedia presentation can help achieve the first two items on the list: education and benefits. The salesperson is going to have to close the sale. But using a multimedia approach has lots of benefits.

- <u>Consistency</u>: If you have a large sales force, each salesperson is delivering a consistent message. Even if you're just on your own, there's a timesaving benefit to making the same presentation (tailored to each specific client) to many prospects.

- <u>Confidence and Image</u>: A good presentation enhances your company's image and instills product confidence. I've had salespeople tell me that their customers feel "good" about our products and our company after seeing a short multimedia presentation.

- <u>Flexibility</u>: For the most part, the computerized authoring tools you'll learn about in this book allow you to easily make changes to your message based on audience feedback or bottom-line results. You're not stuck with an inflexible "canned" presentation. You can even change your presentation on the fly while you're giving it, to answer specific questions or to meet the needs of a specific audience.

Summing Up Sales Presentations

For the most part, multimedia sales presentations are:

- <u>Linear</u>: They go from beginning (education) to middle (benefits) to end (close) in a straight line.

- <u>Scripted</u>: The salesperson learns a script that tracks the presentation and adds his or her personality to the script after becoming familiar with it.

They come in two basic flavors: scripted-portable and interactive. (*Learn more about these presentation types in Chapts. 3 and 4.*)

- <u>Scripted-portable</u>: The salesperson can make the presentation in the prospect's home or office, in one-on-one scenarios or to a large group.

- <u>Interactive</u>: The salesperson sends a self-paced interactive (or scripted video) presentation to help prequalify a prospect.

Marketing Presentations

Marketing presentations set the stage for future sales presentations that result in "design-wins," high-tech marketing jargon for closing a sale and getting the product designed in. You watch marketing presentations on television every day, touting everything from automobiles to xylophones - they're known as *advertisements*.

Using the software authoring tools and techniques presented in this book, <u>you</u> can produce extremely sophisticated television-quality commercials right on your desktop! These productions can combine graphics, animation, audio, and video in one powerful presentation designed to pull attention to your company and its products or to a specific product.

The next time you go to a trade show, look around at the way other companies use multimedia presentations in their kiosks to draw attention to their products. Imitation is the greatest form of flattery, so imitate (never plagiarize).

Interactive and Self-Running Presentations

At our last major trade show, our company used multimedia with excellent results. As I mentioned earlier, the company I work for offers a wide variety of "software tools" used by engineers designing integrated circuits. We strategically placed computer terminals around the periphery of our display area. Each computer terminal contained an interactive presentation that allowed the engineer to select one of our products from a menu. It then took the viewer on a guided tour of the selected product. The tour was both self-paced and interactive, allowing the user to move around inside our software and explore it to almost any depth desired. He our she could get a quick overview, or venture deeper to see how specific, complex tasks are performed.

We had a large-screen display near the center of our kiosk that presented our unified message, the corporate story, and a product overview. This tied our show display together, while the hands-on approach gave our prospective customers the "feel" of our products. Of course, multimedia isn't an end unto itself. We wouldn't have been successful without knowledgable account engineers and marketing specialists on hand to field customer questions.

Scripted Marketing Presentations

An effective way to get your message out is to use a scripted marketing presentation. This is very similar to a scripted sales presentation, except the content is directed toward building confidence in your product or company that will bolster and aid your sales force, rather than closing the sale. Scripted marketing presentations are usually not given one-on-one. They are usually made before a large audience or put onto videotape and widely distributed. New product announcements and overviews and competitive comparisons are two ideal candidates for scripted marketing presentations.

One large multinational electronics company uses scripted presentations to give its direct sales force and distributorships information about its latest products. The presentations show how to effectively present these products, and what the competition offers. I've put together programs for them that include scripted marketing modules that are sent to the field and presented by the office manager at each distributorship. Then, at their annual meeting, I produce another series of scripted presentations to be used in an auditorium setting.

Marketing Presentations: The Bottom Line

Marketing presentations tend to be aimed at a very large and broad audience, either at major trade shows, directly to a large customer base, or to many salespeople who use the information to help close sales and increase market share. All three basic types of presentations can be used to accomplish these missions:

- Scripted: A scripted presentation is perfect for delivering a message to a large audience. The material is well organized and can be rehearsed in advance to ensure a perfect presentation. Scripted presentations can also be sent to the field to be given by office managers to their sales force. Sending a scripted presentation to the field is one way of multiplying its reach and effectiveness.

- Interactive: Interactive presentations allow a select audience to learn about your company and its products in a self-paced interactive way. Interactive presentations offer the ability to explore to a depth that suits individual needs. An interactive presentation can deliver a highly personalized message to an extremely broad and diversified audience, making it an excellent vehicle for trade shows.

- Self-Running: Complete message productions make perfect centerpieces at trade show kiosks, and can also be packaged on either computer disk or videotape to send to a broad customer base.

Training Presentations

Multimedia training presentations help the teacher communicate his or her point quickly, and in a way that sticks in the student's mind. Just using simple graphics can make a memorable impression.

In premultimedia days when I was going to high school, one teacher used an attention-grabbing technique to heighten our interest in biology and set the stage for the rest of the year's studies. On day one she walked into the classroom holding a brown paper bag. Without saying a word she stepped up to the lab sink at the front of the class. She reached into the paper bag, grabbed a handful of helicopterlike seed pods, tossed them into the air, and let them spin down around us. We were stunned, amazed, and silenced. Then she said, "Isn't nature wonderful?" That graphic display really made me sit up and take notice. I paid close attention to her during the balance of the year, never quite sure when she was going to put on another amazing display.

A well-crafted multimedia presentation can have the same effect on your students. It can grab their attention and keep them interested and excited about learning. *Don't overuse and abuse the special-effects side of your presentation. When you do, you dilute its effectiveness.* You have to find a balance between the material and the effects to keep your students on the edge of their seats. This axiom is true for all multimedia presentations, but it is especially true for training presentations.

As a teacher, you want your students to absorb the material and really understand it so they can apply it effectively in their lives. Experiential learning, where the student interacts in the learning experience rather than being lectured, is extremely effective. Interactive multimedia training presentations are one way to make this happen; a creative mix of multimedia presentation and hands-on learning is another effective learning methodology.

Scripted Seminar Training

The traditional lecture hall setting where a professor moves about on a stage scribbling incomprehensibly on a blackboard in front of a large note-taking audience is still with us today. It doesn't have to be. Seminar-style multimedia training presentations can wake up the audience and help make even the most complex topic fun and exciting to learn. Learning chemistry and the periodic tables showing full-color animated atoms sure beats looking at yellowed paper charts, and the power to make these types of presentations is as close as your PC, as you'll see in Chap. 3, *"Scripted Presentations."*

The learning setting doesn't have to be a school's classroom or lecture hall. In today's world of powerful-but-complex technology, more and more corporations are offering training courses to their customers. For example, Macromedia Corporation, the developer and manufacturer of DIRECTOR (one of the multimedia authoring tools you'll learn about is in Chapter 3) offers , on-site interactive training courses that teach how to get the most out of their products. Virtually all manufacturers of high-end software products offer these types of courses either on-site or at their customer's location. Training has become a necessary adjunct and profit center for many leading-edge companies.

Many of these companies are still teaching advanced graphical software use with black-and-white overhead slides. I went to a conference last year and attended a seminar about multimedia extensions to a company's software - it was presented using text-only, black-and-white overhead slides!

Needless to say, they didn't convince me (or the audience) that they had actually entered the world of multimedia. How could we take them seriously?

A scripted multimedia presentation, where the teacher narrates and controls the presentation's pace, is an ideal way to present complex topics in a corporate or classroom setting. You can apply this technique to any training challenge to teach about virtually any topic - from complex software operation to marketing strategies to inorganic chemistry.

A well-crafted, seminar-style multimedia presentation lets you make the impact of throwing seeds into the air without having to clean up the mess.

Reach Out Globally with Interactive Training

You can expand the reach and effectiveness of your training by producing interactive presentations that can be handed to students to work on at home, mailed to them, or transmitted directly to their computers over a global electronic network. Regardless of which delivery system you choose, interactive presentations are an effective way of getting your students really involved in the learning process in a hands-on way.

One company's customer service department sends interactive multimedia presentations in response to customers' questions about their software. This presentation on computer disk first guides the customer through the operation of the section of software that the user is having a problem with, then lets him or her explore the entire tool in interactive, self-paced fashion.

Any training application, whether it is teaching how a tractor works, how to grow rice on arid land, how to use a product or service, or how to be an effective trainer, can be taught effectively using interactive multimedia. It gets your students directly involved.

Watching and Learning

Although the best ways to learn are through interaction with a teacher or experientially, students can learn by simply watching a presentation. You can use self-running presentations, with no interaction, to give an overview of the operation of anything from a mechanical device or software to a service or investment concept.

Training Presentation Wrap-up

Teaching is the art of effectively conveying information to students so that every student leaves the training with knowledge that he or she can apply in the real world. The tools and techniques you'll learn about in this book can give you an edge and help you to become an even more effective teacher. In summary, multimedia training presentations can be produced and given in any of the three basic presentation styles.

- Scripted: A scripted presentation is perfect for delivering a message in a seminar setting. It offers the impact that keeps students interested and anxious to learn more. The material is well organized and can be rehearsed in advance to ensure a perfect presentation. Using multimedia, the teacher can change direction during the training in response to student questions, or can tailor the presentation for different audiences before the training begins.

- Interactive: Interactive presentations allow students to learn at their own pace in an experiential and interactive way that reinforces the learning process.

With the advent of the Internet, you can now distribute interactive learning modules to students around the globe.

- <u>Self-Running</u>: Although not as powerful as scripted or interactive presentations, self-running presentations can teach by showing how things are done and how things work. Some museums use self-running presentations, usually on videotape, to give a narrated overview of specific displays.

Delivering the Corporate Message

More and more corporations are using multimedia techniques to get the message out to their shareholders. At shareholder meetings, seminar-style presentations, similar to those used by marketing, are used by the corporate officers to present the "big picture" to a large audience. Whether you're talking about big money at a shareholder's meeting or looking for financing for a start-up, *you and your company are going to be judged by the quality of the presentation.* The result you want is investor confidence. Granted, you can get up and deliver your message with absolutely no props, just pure oratory force. But visual and audio accompaniment used correctly will amplify your message and make it resonate in your audience's heads. When you use appropriate multimedia techniques, your audience <u>will</u> remember your presentation, for better or for worse, so its content and how you present it are extremely important.

Internet, WorldWide Web, and the Corporate Message

Technology is moving so rapidly that corporate publications are no longer limited to traditional paper magazines. They can use multimedia techniques to bring their message alive in full color with sound, video, and animation and take advantage of electronic networks to distribute it worldwide.

Internet, a worldwide electronic network, now includes a hypertext-hypermedia system called WorldWide Web that lets users navigate the global Internet

·system with a simple click of a mouse. WorldWide Web hypertext documents, like annual reports or corporate magazines, contain embedded text links to other documents that are located on computer servers worldwide. If this book were a WWW hypertext document, and you wanted to learn more about the history of Worldwide Web, you'd simply click the underlined text and a document containing WWW's history would appear on your screen.

Taking this concept one step forward, software tools like Adobe Acrobat deliver full-color brochures directly to desktops around the globe to revolutionize the way people produce, deliver, and browse documentation.

The Ultimate Interactive Multimedia Presentation

Hypermedia, also a feature of World-Wide Web, takes hypertext one step further. Clicking a hypermedia hot spot on a document links you to sounds, images, animation, and movies. If this page were your computer screen, clicking on this icon would display a motion picture, complete with sound.

Hypermedia's uses are boundless. You're no longer limited to delivering your message on a one-dimensional paper surface. For example, a company's president could deliver the corporate message in an audio/movie embedded in an on-line corporate report. Or you could use animated pie graphs or column charts to show your company's growth. When a company wants to present a new product, or show how a complex product works, hypermedia on the Internet is ready to help deliver the message – powerfully, in a way that was technologically impossible until now. This emerging media provides the platform for the ultimate interactive multimedia presentation.

The same tools and techniques you'll learn about in this book to produce multimedia presentations are used to produce the material for the global Net. The presentation is the same; only the delivery system is different.

A Welcome Message from the Boss

I scripted a multimedia presentation that included an introduction from the company's president. A video of the president appeared in the screen's center at the opening of the presentation. He introduced himself, then pointed to each of the four corners of the screen in turn. When he pointed to the upper-left corner of the screen a picture of the corporate headquarters appeared; he spoke about this, then pointed to the upper-right corner and presented the executive officers. The third and fourth corners of the screen showed the company's product and people. This type of on-screen interaction is just one technique that can make your corporate presentations stand out. You'll learn more in Chaps. 3 and 4.

Covering All the Corporate Bases

Here's a short checklist of some corporate and financial multimedia applications to help get your creative juices flowing:

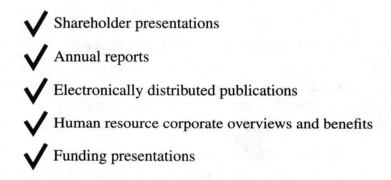

✓ Shareholder presentations

✓ Annual reports

✓ Electronically distributed publications

✓ Human resource corporate overviews and benefits

✓ Funding presentations

Corporate Image Summary

- <u>Scripted</u>: A scripted presentation is perfect for delivering your message at a large shareholder's meeting or for a funding presentation. Use scripted multimedia to make a one-on-one funding presentation in the investment banker's office-right at his or her computer.

- Interactive: Interactive on-line publications are the corporate communications wave of the future. Using interactive multimedia, you reach out to an enormous audience and touch each viewer in an individual and personalized way. Interactive presentations are also perfect for self-guided company tours that allow the user to explore the corporation's structure, products, and employees in a self-paced way.

- Self-Running: Human resource departments can use self-running presentations (on computer disk or video) to present a corporate overview, including benefits packages, to prospective employees. The corporate message can also be produced on video and distributed to shareholders, investment bankers, employees, or anyone else the corporation wants to get the word out to. The corporate message can also be given at trade shows using self-running presentations.

Getting Down to Business

Now that you've seen how powerful multimedia is and had a chance to think about how you'd like to use it to get your message across, move on to the next two chapters to learn how to develop and script your multimedia production!

Laying the Foundation

The fundamental multimedia presentation is a *scripted presentation* – you follow a script and control the presentation's pace. It's much like a traditional overhead slide presentation, but with the added impact of color graphics and animation projected in front of an audience or directly on a computer's screen. Essentially, scripted presentations are fancy slide shows. Complementary text moves onto the screen as you and/or the presenter talk about each point. This animated text, accompanied by animated charts, graphs, and graphic illustrations, makes the point and helps the viewer retain the information. The presenter supplies the sound! Understanding and using scripted presentations lay the foundation for multimedia success.

Before you can produce and give a good presentation you have to write a good script. The script forms the framework upon which all presentations are built – the stronger you build this underlying structure, the stronger and more powerful the presentation. You begin building a script by asking questions about the presentation's audience, the message you want to deliver, and the way you want to deliver it. Once these questions are answered, you develop an outline or storyboard, then write the script. It is vitally important to schedule review and feedback after each major step to keep your presentation on track.

Figure 3.1   Scripting a presentation.

This chapter takes you step by step through the creation of a typical scripted presentation and shows you valuable techniques you can use when you script your presentation (Fig. 3.1).

The Two Fundamentals

Keep these two fundamental points in mind as you write your outline and script.

1. <u>Make your presentation short, simple, and right to the point</u>. As a general rule of thumb, limit your scripted presentation to no more than 20 or 30 minutes. Plan for approximately 20 to 25 slides (figuring around 1 minute on the average for each slide, with some slack time for audience questions).

    For the most part, scripted presentations (except when central to a training program) are used to deliver an overview of a product or service. One application, mentioned in Chap. 2, is to qualify prospects. In all cases, you want to deliver the most information in the shortest possible time. Also, when more than one speaker is presenting material at a show or conference, each speaker is usually allocated 30 minutes for their presentation. A 20-minute scripted limit leaves time for audience interaction.

    > If you are producing technical or sales training, you can treat each portion of the training as discrete, 30-minute modules and script each module following the scripting guidelines and examples shown later in this chapter.

2. <u>Focus on important points repeatedly, in different ways</u>, throughout the presentation to ensure that your audience gets the message. Don't be afraid to repeat a point as long as it's the message you want your audience to absorb.

Information for Your Presentation

When I'm crafting a presentation for a client, I take my tape recorder with me to our first meeting and ask about the topic and the main point he or she wants to make. I also find out who the audience is so I can tailor the presentation to custom fit. For example, a presentation aimed at salespeople has a different content and tone than a presentation aimed at engineers. After we determine the audience, I ask questions designed to get as much information as possible for that audience.

Be prepared: bring a notebook (or notebook computer) to the kickoff meeting with your questions written in, and plenty of blank space for notes below each question. Then just push RECORD on your tape recorder and begin the interview. Take lots of notes – <u>never</u> rely only on your tape recorder! I lost a full hour's interview when I didn't realize that the tape was in backward – operator error – but very costly!

Sample Questions

I've put together two lists of questions to help you get started, one set aimed at a technical sales audience, the other aimed at engineers. Major categories, listed in capital letters, will help you tailor these questions to fit almost any audience.

Sales Audience

- AUDIENCE PROFILE. Profile of the salespeople toward whom this presentation is aimed.

    - Are they very technically oriented or only peripherally concerned with technical details?

    - What turns them on? What motivates them? Usually it's the bottom line – show how the product puts money in their pockets and they're all ears! (This is a good way to begin the presentation! Get their attention up front.)

- PRESENTATION PROFILE. Will this presentation be made one-on-one, or before a group?

- PRESENTATION OBJECTIVE – WHAT YOU WANT TO CREATE. What are your goals? What do you want the salespeople to do as a result of this presentation?

    - How do you want your audience to use the information in the presentation?

- AUDIENCE-SPECIFIC INFORMATION. Who is the competition and how do we stack up against them?

    - Pricewise

    - Featurewise

    - Name recognition

    - Upward compatibility

    - Support services

- FEATURES. What does the product do or how do you use it?

    - What are the product's features?

- BENEFITS. What are the product's benefits to the customer?

- PRODUCT END-USER PROFILE. What is a typical customer profile?

    - Are they manufacturers?

    - Are they researchers?

    - Are they more interested in cost or do they need state-of-the-art performance regardless of price?

    - What are they using now for a solution?

    - Are they buying our company's products now or are the salespeople going to be calling on mostly new prospects?

- APPLICATIONS. How are these customers going to use the product?

    - List of applications

- AVAILABILITY. What is the availability of the product?

    - Lead times

- COMPATIBILITY. How does this product tie in with your other products?

- ORDERING INFORMATION. Includes items such as:

    - Part numbers

    - Price

    - Procedure

    - Terms

- SUPPORT. What product support is available?

Engineering Audience

If you are aiming at an engineering audience, the basic set of questions is a variation on the sales questions:

- AUDIENCE PROFILE. Describe the profile of the engineers for whom this presentation is designed.

  What depth of knowledge do you want to impart to them? Is this just an overview, or are you planning to craft a complete training program? What are your goals? What do you want the engineers to do with the information?
- PRESENTATION PROFILE. Is this going to be one-on-one or in a seminar setting?
- RELEVANT TECHNICAL INFORMATION. Sketch a block or flow diagram that overviews the product's operation.

  - You can use a rendering of this, and other engineering drawings, in your presentation

- PRESENTATION FOCUS. Review the specification highlighting technical <u>benefits</u> and <u>features</u> that you feel are important and want emphasized.

  - Always get a copy of the specification, manual, and all other relevant technical information as background for your presentation

- PRODUCT END-USER PROFILE. How can engineers make the best use of your product?

  - How can they design it into their system?

  - How can they use it?

- TOOLS and SUPPORT. What tools are available to help the engineer use your product more effectively?
- What training and other support are available for this product

  - Documentation

  - Training courses

  - Technical support

The information from your interview forms the basis of your presentation.

Outline First!   # IMPORTANT

Preparing a detailed outline is extremely critical. It charts your presentation's direction and gives you a chance to run it by your client for review and approval before you go marching off in the wrong direction. Take the time to do a thorough outline. A well-crafted outline saves you time in the long run by providing a clear direction. When you write your script, all you have to do is fill in the blanks.

Begin by structuring your outline into three basic chunks of information:

- <u>Beginning</u>. Introduce the presentation.

    - The presentation directed at salespeople begins by briefly introducing the product, tells them that it will increase their sales, and tells them what they can expect in the rest of the presentation.

- <u>Middle</u>. Overview the product and present related sales strategies.

    - The middle section of the presentation describes the product and can include information about how to sell the product, what <u>features</u> to emphasize, what types of customers will make good prospects, how the product will <u>benefit</u> them, what techniques the salesperson can use to close the deal, and information about the competition.

- <u>End</u>

    - The last portion of the presentation can review the <u>features</u> of the product and the <u>benefits</u> to the customer, talks about intangibles like customer product support of the product, and then moves onto the closing slides.

    - The final slides can contain a brief summary of the entire presentation, followed by a "call to action" slide, and a closing slide that summarizes the company's other products and strengths.

For scripted presentations, a traditional outline works perfectly. Later, when we delve into *self-running* and *interactive* presentations, you'll see how an outline plus a storyboard helps you to visualize the presentation's flow. When I craft an outline, I visualize graphics that complement the point I want to make in each slide. Then I describe my graphic ideas on paper. If you think better by drawing your ideas on paper or on a computer screen, by all means do it. Do whatever helps you to organize and plan your presentation. The idea is to know as much as possible about the final product <u>before</u> you produce it.

Guidelines to Effective Presentation Creation

Put this list of guidelines in front of you as you craft your presentation:

- Before you begin, make sure you know exactly what you want to communicate.

- Make sure that every slide you create adds to the presentation's impact. Consolidate, move, or eliminate slides that don't move the presentation forward.

- Use a template for consistent type style and background color. Use your creative eye for graphic placement and effects.

- Keep each slide as simple as possible. Don't clutter! It's often better to break a message into two or more slides rather than try to cram too much on one slide.

- Keep effects to a minimum. Use them only to emphasize <u>important</u> points. Don't let your message get lost in overused animation, sound, and special effects. Remember, <u>your</u> message is <u>the</u> message.

A Sample Scripted Presentation

The following scripted presentation is aimed at technical salespeople. I took this example from a presentation I prepared for a multinational electronics firm's sales force. It was produced using Microsoft's *PowerPoint* presentation software to allow us the flexibility of showing it on computer, with animated text and graphics, and as overhead slides. We designed the presentation to motivate distribution salespeople to sell a new technical product to new and existing accounts by giving them the incentive and ammunition they needed. Here's this presentation's basic flow:

BEGINNING
• Warm-up
• Introduction
• Product positioning
• Product description/features
MIDDLE
• Features, benefits, and sales tips
• Competitive information
• Feature and benefit summaries
END
• Product support
• Sales strategy summary and call to action
• Company strengths and close

I've added explanatory "slide" notes at the bottom of each slide so you can focus on the presentation's organization without getting thrown off by the technical jargon in the script.

Plug and Play

The important thing to look for in this presentation is flow and organization. Use it as a template as you craft your presentation. Plug your ideas into the template's structure and you are on your way to top-notch productions.

Presentation

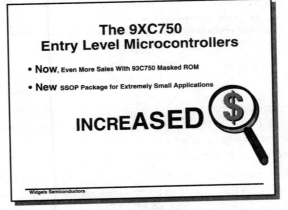

Slide 1
Warm-up - Getting Audience Interested

Script:

Widget Semiconductors now makes it possible for you to enter the low-end microcontroller marketplace with two exciting new products: the 97C750 OTP and 93C750 Masked ROM entry level microcontrollers.

Slide 2
Introduction

Script:

This short 20 minute presentation will introduce you to the exciting 9XC750s, show you the potential in the market place, and give you the background and information you need to increase your sales with this low memory part.

With the introduction of the 97X750 OTP and Masked ROM micros, Widget has expanded the memory offered in its microcontrollers from an industry high of 32K of ROM all the way down to 1K. Building on the success of our 97C751, this low-end part opens up a whole world of sales possibilities for you.

Speaker's Note:

This presentation is scripted. But, that doesn't mean that you should read it word-for-word. The best way to give a powerful and effective talk is by being yourself. Rehearse with the script, then use your own words and phrasing during the actual presentation.

**A Quick Look at Widgets'
Low Cost Derivatives**

	ROM	RAM	I/O	SERIAL COM.	# of TIMERS	FEATURES
80C51	4k	128	32	UART	2	40-Pin
9XC75	2K	64	19	I²C	1	A to D, 28-PIN
9XC751	2k	64	19	I²C	1	24-Pin Skinny Dip Pkg.

Now... Introducing 9XC750

Widgets Semiconductors

**Slide 3
Product Positioning**

Script:

Widget Semiconductors leads the market by offering more derivative devices than any other manufacturer. The number of derivatives exceeds 40 devices (our competitors offer less than 10). This allows designers to closely match their design needs for optimal control performance. Widget leads with high-end microcontrollers, and has broadened this lead with its low-cost 9XC751 and 9XC752 derivatives in response to customer requests for smaller memory devices and lower cost devices.

The 9XC751 and 9XC752 microcontrollers are ideal for applications that require only 2K of program space. This family uses less board area and offers features not available on the 90C51. Their smaller memory and fewer I/Os result in a lower component cost. And, because they're CMOS devices, they draw low power too!

To complement these families we've introduced an exciting new entry into the low-cost arena - the 9XC750 microcontrollers. The 97X750 is one case where less is better, as you'll see in this presentation.

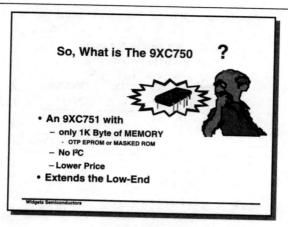

Slide 4
Product Description

Script:

The 9XC750 has the same architecture and has a smaller memory
and fewer features than the 9XC751 and '752. But, the 9XC750
only has 1K-Byte of either OTP or Masked ROM memory, a 16-
bit timer, a 24-pin package, and is the lowest cost OTP microcontroller in the Widget line-up.

The 9XC750 extends Widget' 8-bit microcontroller line down to
meet your customers' low price microcontroller needs.

Slide 5
Product Feature and Benefit

Script:

For customers who need super-fast processing speed, the 97C750 is the FIRST and ONLY 1K, low-cost 8-bit OTP 40MHz micro-controller on the market - you have NO competition! And, when your customer moves into high-volume production, he can move into it using the 40MHz 93C750 Masked ROM part.

The 9XC750's 40MHz operating frequency translates into a 300 nanosecond instruction cycle time. Plus, it performs benchmark 8 x 8 multiply arithmetic operations in a blazing 1.2 microseconds!

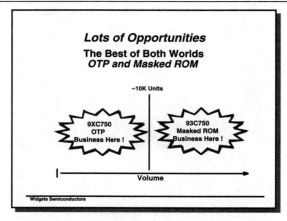

Slide 6
Product Benefit

Script:

The majority of microcontroller applications are produced in moderate quantities. The 9XC750 is positioned perfectly to meet this market's needs. The 97C750's low cost, coupled with the flexibility of its OTP design, make it perfect for moderate production runs. Then, when quantities get higher, you can move your customer right in to the lower cost Masked ROM 93C750.

The 9XC750 Opens New Doors for You
Your Entrè Into New Accounts

9XC750

- **Low cost**
  - Competitive with many ASICs and FPGAs
- **Small 24-pin In-line Package & Tiny SSOP Surface Mount Package**
- **1K EPROM = Opportunities**

Move up From ASICs & FPGAs
to Microcontroller Power!

Widgets Semiconductors

Slide 7
Sales Tips

Script:

Accounts that were once out of reach because they use ASICs, FPGAs or other low-end microcontrollers are now viable prospects. The 9XC750's low cost, its OTP and Masked ROM flexibility, small 24-pin DIP and SSOP packages, and full 80C51 instruction set make it ideal for breaking into those once unaccessible accounts.

Speakers Note:

The 9XC750 unit price in quantity is below $3, making it ideal for a world of low-end applications. The 93C750 is even lower! (Low $1 price range.)

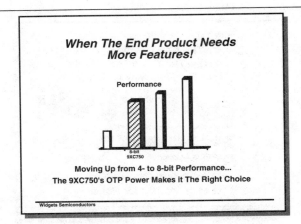

Slide 8
Customer Benefits

Script:

The 9XC750 is priced right for customers who want to move up to the power of 8-bit performance. At more than 40% below the cost of a typical microcontroller, the 9XC750 is a real bargain.

And, the 9XC750 offers the flexibility of low-cost OTP. This means that your customers can move up to 8-bit power with their new designs. They'll get fast time to market, and the flexibility of being able to make changes as their new design evolves.

The 9XC750 narrows the gap between 4- and 8-bit, and is ideal for customers who are just entering the market or who are upgrading their product line.

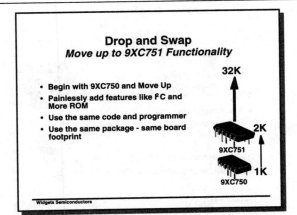

Slide 9
Customer Benefits

Script:

Your customers can begin with the 9XC750. Then when their application requires more features and increased program space, all they have to do is drop in an 9XC751 part and swap out the 97C750 - they've just added I2C-bus and doubled the ROM.

Both devices use the same code, the same programmer, are available in the same 24-pin package, and they're both members of the same familiar micro family.

Also, and very importantly, your customers can use the 97C750 OTP micro during development and in initial production. Then when quantities get really high, costs can be lowered dramatically by replacing it with a masked ROM 93C750.

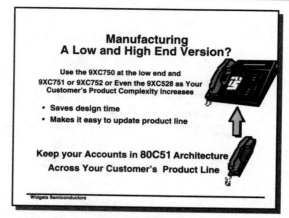

**Manufacturing
A Low and High End Version?**

Use the 9XC750 at the low end and
9XC751 or 9XC752 or Even the 9XC528 as Your
Customer's Product Complexity Increases

- Saves design time
- Makes it easy to update product line

**Keep your Accounts in 80C51 Architecture
Across Your Customer's Product Line**

Widgets Semiconductors

Slide 10
Customer Benefits

Script:

If your customer is manufacturing or planning to manufacture both high- and low-end versions of the same device, they can use the 9XC750 for the low-end version and other 80C51 derivative microcontrollers for the high-end versions - the ones with all those bells and whistles.

Using 80C51 derivative product from the low to the high end lets your customers take advantage of the same architecture and the same code for all their product versions.

Working with the same familiar architecture over the entire product line saves engineering time and money, and makes it easy to program revisions and updates as the product evolves.

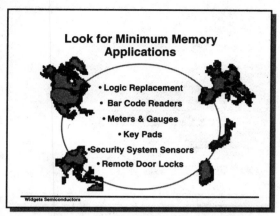

Slide 11
Applications

Script:

Look for low-end, minimum memory applications.

These applications just touch the surface. Look for applications that need the power of a microcontroller but are not memory intensive.

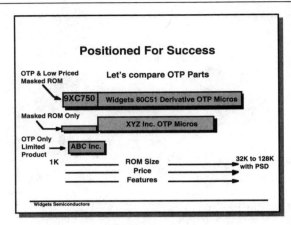

Slide 12
Competition

Script:

The 9XC750 is competitively positioned against XYZ's OTP parts at the low-end (they don't offer a 1K OTP part), and as a member of the Widget family the 9XC750 gives your customers a stepping stone up to higher memory and more features. Features like serial interfaces, AtoD and DtoA converters, on chip memory up to 32K, Flash Memory. And now with the addition of our X series of peripheral micros, you can offer your customers memory up to 128 kilobytes!

And, for applications requiring high speed, the 9XC750 at 40 MHz blows the socks off the competition.

ABC Inc. is another player in the low-end OTP market, but they only offer 1 and 2K parts. This limited family decreases their market and increases our opportunity at accounts that want to move up in the same architecture as their products become more sophisticated.

9XC750
Feature Summary

- All the benefits of OTP and Masked ROM
- Small Package Size
- Available with 40MHz Speed
- Low cost

Widgets Semiconductors

Slide 13
Feature Summary

Script:

The 9XC750 is a bare-bones 8-bit microcontroller, but it has lots of features that make it easy for your customers to design it into their products.

- OPT gets new products up and running fast - right into production.
- Small, .300" 24-pin package fits into tight places, and is also perfect for upgrading from 4-bit components.
- Subminiature SSOP package for today's mobile marketplace.
- It's available in a 30 MHz version for customers who need a low-cost micro with blazing speed.

It's low cost, typically less than $3 for the 97C750 OTP version and in the low $1 range for the 93C750 EPROM, make it perfect for entry level applications or for migration up from 4-bit or logic devices. (Remember, 4-bit devices don't come in OTP versions - our low cost 8-bit parts do!)

9XC750 Customer Benefits Summary

- One architecture for all applications and versions
- Great entry-level product
- The flexibility of inexpensive OTP &
  high volume low cost Masked ROM
- More processing power than 4-bit or logic devices
- Full range of 80C51 development tools
- Proven and familiar architecture

Widgets Semiconductors

Slide 14
Benefit Summary

Script:

The 9XC750 offers a whole range of exciting benefits to your customers. Use these points when talking to prospects to expand your accounts and increase sales in your territory.

Speakers Notes:

Read and embellish slide bullets.

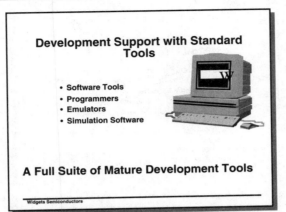

Development Support with Standard Tools

- Software Tools
- Programmers
- Emulators
- Simulation Software

A Full Suite of Mature Development Tools

Widgets Semiconductors

Slide 15
Support

Script:

As a member of the extensive Widget family, the 9XC750 uses all the programmers, emulators, simulators and much of the same software coding as its feature-rich relatives.

Your customers can start evaluation with our low-cost Emulator/ Simulator, and may use a wide selection of powerful development tools.

9XC750 Sales Strategy
Low Cost - High Value - Flexibility

- Find applications that need the Power of an 80C51 but with little memory and few features
- Capture 4-bit migration
- ENTRY level 80C51 derivative
- Compete with PICs and low-end Motorola micros
- Sell Upgradeability - Pin-for-pin Compatible with 751
- Stress the value of OTP and the Cost savings of Masked ROM

Widgets Semiconductors

Slide 16
Sales Strategy Summary &
Call to Action!

Script:

Review the above bullets, then...

Just find applications that need microcontroller power, with little memory and few features, and you've found a new account or expanded an existing one.

The Most Microcontrollers

in the

W 🌍 rld

Widgets Semiconductor 8-Bit Microcontrollers

Widgets Semiconductors

Slide 17
Company Strengths
Close

Script:

Widget Semiconductors is the only company that offers the 9XC750 - an 8-bit microcontroller with the power and price that make it easy for you to move up to 8-bit performance. We offer unique and innovative product features to bring you THE MOST 8-BIT MICROCONTROLLERS IN THE WORLD.

Here are just some of the many Widget Semiconductors features:

Bulleted list of products with features and benefits of each.

Regardless of your needs, Widget Semiconductors has the right microcontroller for the job. We offer the most 8-bit microcontrollers in the world!

Choosing Authoring Software

About the Widgets Scripted Presentation

This scripted presentation was produced and presented using Microsoft PowerPoint authoring and presentation software. We could have chosen to produce and present using other excellent packages such as Aldus Persuasion, Gold Disk Astound or *Animation Works Interactive,* or Asymetrix COMPEL. However, we elected to use PowerPoint primarily because our client, "Widget Semiconductors," uses PowerPoint to produce overhead slides and is familiar with its operation. They asked us to produce this presentation in PowerPoint to give them the ability to make their own last-minute edits and updates.

PowerPoint is an excellent tool, and includes PowerPoint Viewer software that allows us to distribute presentations worldwide, even for play on computers that don't have the PowerPoint program installed. It also ports seamlessly between Macintosh and MS-DOS/Windows-based computers, allowing us to work on and modify the presentation on either platform.

All the presentation packages we use include a graphics library. PowerPoint's library of more than 500 pictures is excellent, as you can see in the previous slides.

Slide and Text Transitions

In a scripted presentation, the presenter provides the sound and controls the presentation's pace. By using the keyboard and/or mouse, the PowerPoint software lets the presenter control each bulleted text line's screen appearances; the timing of each slide's transition, and allows the presenter to move back to review previous slides or jump to specific slides during the presentation.

All these features are not unique to PowerPoint. Many of these capabilities, and more, are included in the other authorware packages overviewed in this book.

Weighing the Considerations

For scripted presentations, you should weigh these considerations when choosing your authoring and presentation software package:

1. Which software is your client using now?
    -   Your client might want you to produce the presentation in a package that suits their needs. Be prepared to be flexible.

2. On which platform (Macintosh or MS-DOS/Windows-based) is the presentation going to be made? Which platform are you going to use to produce your presentations?
    -   It is always best to produce the presentation on a computer system that you're familiar with, and to have the capability of presenting it on either Macintosh or MS-DOS/Window-based computers. (As *Power PC* computers grow in acceptance, this consideration will eventually fade.)

3. What level of animation do you want to use in your presentation? Do you want animated charts and graphs? Objects that move about the screen? Or do you want to keep it simple with just movable text and a simple animation?
    -   Some authorware packages include built-in animation. However, <u>all</u> the authoring/presentation software listed in this book allows you to import and present animation, movies, and sound.
    -   With packages like PowerPoint and Aldus Persuasion, you can produce interesting animation effects by manipulating the transition effects between slides. Other packages, like Gold Disk's Animation Works Interactive and Astound, Asymetrix's COMPEL, and Macromedia's Macromedia Action include sophisticated built-in animation capabilities.

Scripted presentations have accompanying speaker notes. Is this capability important to you? Some of the packages that offer advanced animation capabilities do not include the ability to write and print speaker notes.

4. Do you want to distribute overhead slides and/or 35mm slides in addition to being able to distribute your presentation for play on a computer?

The Decision Process

The best rule of thumb for any presentation is to keep it simple. This is especially true when it comes to scripted presentations where the presenter provides the narration and control. However, you may want to include on-screen point-and-click interaction during your presentation and may absolutely need this and other advanced capabilities. The bottom line when selecting an authoring package is that it meets your needs, and helps you get your message across efficiently and effectively.

The best way to choose your primary authoring/presentation software is as follows:

- Do a needs assessment.

- Read about the software packages that most closely meet your needs.

- Get more information directly from the software manufacturer or from a local dealer.

- Get demonstration software or videotape that gives you a better feel for your selection's capabilities. (Most commercial on-line services, like American On Line and Compuserve, feature a multimedia section that includes many demonstration programs you can download and try out.)

Once you make a selection it should be the right one for you and your job. The software you use affects the look, flexibility, and impact of your presentations. Take your time!

Authorware Comparison Table

Table 3.1 alphabetically lists some software packages you can use to produce and give scripted presentations. Use it to help you zero in on the products that most closely meet your needs, then read about your choice in Chap. 4. (Not every software package listed is overviewed.

TABLE 3.1 Presentation and Authoring Software

Name	Macintosh	Windows	Player/viewer	Speaker notes	O/H slides	Transition effects	Full animation	On-screen interactive
Action!	YES	YES	YES	NO	NO	YES	YES	YES
Aldus Persuasion	YES	YES	NO	YES	YES	YES	NO	NO
Animation Works Interactive	NO	YES	YES	NO	NO	YES	YES	YES
Astound	YES	YES	YES	YES	YES	YES	YES	YES
COMPEL	NO	YES	YES	YES	YES	YES	YES	YES
PowerPoint	YES	YES	YES	YES	YES	YES	NO	NO

Table 3.1 Explained

Here's an explanation of each column[1]:

- **Macintosh/Windows**: Primary development and viewing platforms.

- **Player/Viewer**: Runtime player or viewer that enables your presentation to be played back on computers that don't have the primary software.

  - For example, you can send a copy of *PowerPoint Viewer* with your presentation to an unlimited number of people who can view it without the *PowerPoint* program installed on their computers.

---

[1] Software packages evolve and improve. This information was accurate when written, but may have changed as you read this book.

- **Speaker Notes**: Printed speaker notes that track each slide in the presentation.

- **O/H Slides**: The capability to print overhead transparencies and/ or 35mm slides.

- **Transition Effects**: Between-slide transition effects like, dissolve, disintegrate, wipe, and box-out.

- **Full Animation**: Built-in animation capability. Although you can import and embed animation into all the listed programs, only those that have built-in animation capabilities are marked YES.

- **On-screen Interactive**: The ability to accept point-and-click mouse input on buttons, hot words/characters, hot icons and other active screen areas to trigger events like animation, sound, or video.

 Every program listed in Table 3.1 allows text to appear on the screen in a variety of ways including flying in from left, right, bottom, or top and materializing.

Moving On

Read Chap. 4 to learn more about production techniques and specific authorware/presentation software packages. Then, after you've purchased your software and produced your presentation, turn to Chap. 5, and get ready to make your first multimedia presentation.

Self-Paced Discovery

An interactive presentation is a dialog between computer and person that empowers the person to explore and discover information at his or her own pace.

The user controls the direction of an interactive presentation by deciding which material is important and making choices on the computer's screen by pointing to an object or portion of text with the cursor and clicking the mouse button or pressing a keyboard key. The computer responds by presenting the requested information.

All interactive authoring and presentation programs have one thing in common: they are all *event -driven*. This means that when an event occurs, a button is pressed, or the cursor wipes over a screen object, something happens in response. (You'll learn more about this later in this chapter as you read about some of the multimedia software packages.)

A well-crafted interactive presentation is an exploratory adventure that allows the user to seek knowledge at any depth you provide. For example, the user can begin learning about a product by reading its general description on the computer's screen; then, by pressing a hypertext link (an underlined or highlighted word or phrase), a button, or an icon, he or she is presented with in-depth information about a specific portion of the product.

Another hallmark of a well-crafted interactive presentation is its ability to keep the user involved and interested. The best interactive presentations include elements of surprise that build excitement and encourage further exploration by presenting different packets of information in different ways:

- Graphically

- Textually

- Using movies

- With narration and sound

- Or all of these elements in combination

Laying the Groundwork

Creating an interactive presentation is a multifaceted job that requires a thorough knowledge of your audience, your topic, and your software tool, coupled with detailed planning. Review Chap. 3 before you begin crafting your presentation. All the points mentioned in that chapter apply here and in preparing for all presentations. Be prepared on these very important points and you will be prepared to craft any presentation well:

- Design your presentation to be easy to operate.

- Gather detailed information about the topic by reading and interviewing.

- Know your audience.

- Know your presentation software's capabilities and limitations.

- Know your message and how to deliver it effectively to your audience.

Choosing an Authoring Tool

Once you know what information and what level of information you are going to present, you are ready to choose an authoring tool that best expresses your message and that:

- You feel comfortable working with

- Plays back on the computer system used by your audience

- Delivers a look and feel that meets your aesthetic requirements

Two Authorware Tool Levels

As shown in Table 4.1, there are essentially two levels of available programs that you can use to create your interactive presentations.

- <u>Level I tools</u> do not use a scripting language, and provide basic slide-to-slide interactivity, usually have some built-in graphics and animation capability, and include the ability to import or link externally created graphics, animation, video, and sound. These tools are easy to learn and are perfect for most business presentation needs.

- Level II tools include all the features of level I tools and also include a scripting language that lets you add flexibility, power, and individualized creativity to your presentation. Scripting-language tools are used by major multimedia CD-ROM producers to create multimedia encyclopedias, exploration-action games, interactive music videos, and more. Using scripting languages takes a bit more time and dedication. But, when customized results are required and you have the time to devote to details, using a scripting language is sometimes the only way to go.

The choice is yours, and to help you make it, this chapter includes short overviews of some effective and popular presentation software packages.

TABLE 4.1 Interactive Authoring Packages

Program name	Manufacturer	Scripting language	Development platform(s)	Playback platform(s)
Level I Authoring Tools				
Action!	Macromedia	None	Macintosh & Windows	Macintosh & Windows
Animation Works Interactive	Gold Disk	None	Windows	Windows
Apple Media Tool	Apple Computer	None	Macintosh	Macintosh & Windows
Astound	Gold Disk	None	Macintosh & Windows	Macintosh & Windows
COMPEL	Asymetrix	None	Windows	Windows

TABLE 4.1 Interactive Authoring Packages

Program name	Manufacturer	Scripting language	Development platform(s)	Playback platform(s)
Level II Authoring Tools				
Apple Media Tool (Programming Environment)	Apple Computer	Apple Media Language	Macintosh	Macintosh & Windows
Director	Macromedia	Lingo[1]	Macintosh	Macintosh & Windows
Multimedia ToolBook	Asymetrix	OpenScript	Windows	Windows

1. Macromedia's Director allows you to author interactive presentations with or without using their scripting language, Lingo.

The Authoring Environment

Some authoring tools have excellent built-in animation capabilities, and some have none. Some of these tools let you accurately time and coordinate events, while others just offer rudimentary timing capabilities. Some tools let you map out your presentation on the screen, while others lack this capability.

Every authoring tool has its strengths and weaknesses, and there is no one tool that is generally better than another. It all depends on what you want to produce and how you like to work.

Later in the chapter you can take a short guided tour of some of these tools to help you decide which one best meets your style and presentation needs.

Figure 4.1 shows a typical level II interactive multimedia presentation authoring tool's capabilities.

Level II tools give the author access to more professional presentation construction options. These types of tools are generally better in the following situations:

- For creating titles for CD distribution

- When you need to port a presentation to a workstation or other high-end environment

- When you need a high level of custom interaction options

- When you just want the added power and flexibility that these tools deliver

Level I tools, on the other hand, typically offer more built-in features, such as the ability to create animations and record sound in the tool. These types of tools are generally better for fast, on-the-fly presentation creation, where you don't absolutely have to handcraft or tailor the look and feel of each presentation to meet a specific need.

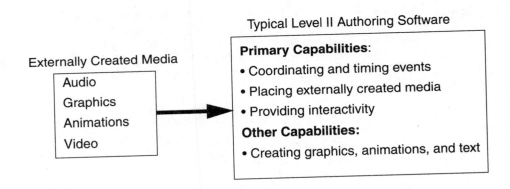

Figure 4.1 *Typical level II interactive multimedia authoring software.*

You'll find an abbreviated tour of all the tools listed in Table 4.1 on page 4-3 and 4-4. You may want to review this table again now, before moving on to the next section, *Designing Your Interactive Presentation.*

Designing Your Interactive Presentation

Each authoring tool allows you to approach interactive design in its own unique way. For example, *Multimedia ToolBook* uses the metaphor of linked hypertext embedded on the pages of a book; the *Apple Media Tool* allows you to graphically link slides together; and *Director* uses a motion-picture studio metaphor, complete with *cast members* and a *studio*, as its design environment. Some higher-end tools, such as *Apple Media Tool*, are more of a place to integrate media you've created using other software packages than for creating artwork and animation. At the other end of the spectrum, *Astound* for example, has built-in facilities that let you produce animations, add and edit sound, import clip art, and create basic drawings.

 NOTE Take your software's nuances into consideration and become familiar with them before you sit down to design your presentation. Once you purchase a software package, take the time to go through the tutorial, and then run the software through its paces by creating a small, but demanding, project to experience its features, capabilities and limitations firsthand.

Even though there are technical and operational differences between each interactive software package, they all have a lot in common:

- They are all event-driven.

- They all include timed-event occurrences.

- They all allow you to design an interactive application that follows a road map of interconnected destinations that you create.

Planning Your Map

You want to create an interactive highway that lets your user navigate easily to whatever level of information he or she is looking for. This typically means going from large ideas or all-encompassing concepts down to the details that make them up. If, for example, you were designing an interactive human anatomy exploration, you'd start with the concept of "body" and work your way down to the cells that make it up – with all the stops in between.

I created an interactive presentation entitled "Hot New Products," aimed at sales engineers that allows them to explore and learn about different electronic components. I wanted them to be able to select any one of five components, then go to that component's "home base" where they can branch out to learn about:

- Technical features

- Customer benefits

- Support tools and personnel

- The competition

- Sample applications

- How to order

Figure 4.2 shows how the upper level of this interactive presentation fits together. Users begin at the opening screen, where he or she selects a component to explore. This takes them to component 1's "home base" where they branch off to explore each feature and benefit in as much depth as desired.

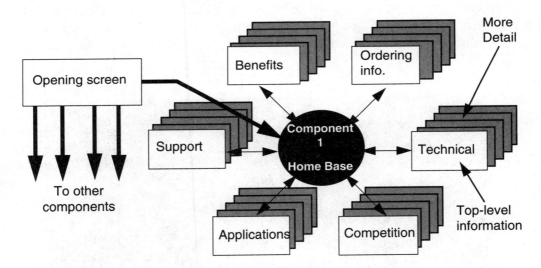

Figure 4.2 Presentation upper-level map.

Two interactive features that aren't shown in Fig. 4.2 are the ability to branch off to explore other components from <u>anywhere</u> in the presentation, and a series of special-effect slides between the "home base" and each topic that adds excitement. I've included a few screen shots of this presentation to show you how it all fits together.

Basic Layout Choices

Your interactive presentation has to fit your audience's needs and personality. Since this presentation was directed at sales engineers, I used the metaphor of a tabbed sales notebook because it would feel comfortable and familiar to them. (This presentation was created and distributed in the Windows environment, using *Multimedia ToolBook*.)

 NOTE *Multimedia ToolBook* supplies a number of templates that you can use as starting places for your presentation. It also provides standard effects, scrolling text windows, buttons, and other prefabricated building blocks that make your job easier. Don't worry! All the authoring and presentation packages give you plenty of material and examples to help you get up and running fast.

The Opening Screen

This screen, with animated revolving globe and flaming "Hot," lets the user press a tab at the bottom of the notebook to explore one of five numbered components. The option to exit is also given here and throughout the presentation (Fig. 4.3).

Figure 4.3 Opening screen.

Home Base

The "home base" screen is the same for each component. The appropriate tab at the bottom of the notebook is highlighted to let the user know which component he or she is exploring (Fig. 4.4).

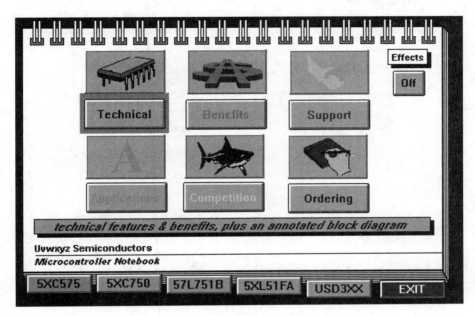

Figure 4.4 Home base.

When the user wipes the cursor across one of the six buttons he or she is told, in the text area below the buttons, what to expect when a highlighted button is pressed. In Fig. 4.4 the Technical button is highlighted, and the message bar tells the user that pressing it leads to "technical features & benefits, plus an annotated block diagram."

The Effects button in the upper-right corner is used to turn special effects on or off. When special effects are On, special surprises occur on the way to each topic. For example, with special effects On, when the Competition button is pressed an animated shark swims toward the viewer. Because this type of surprise is "neat" the first time around but may get in the way after that, I give the user the option of turning special effects Off.

The Technical Section

The Technical section shown in Fig. 4.5 is typical of the many destinations the user can select. Once here, the user further explores by selecting a button which displays scrolling text, as shown in Fig. 4.6. Also, in this window the user can go to a Block Diagram of the component where he or she can point and click on a subcomponent and see its function displayed.

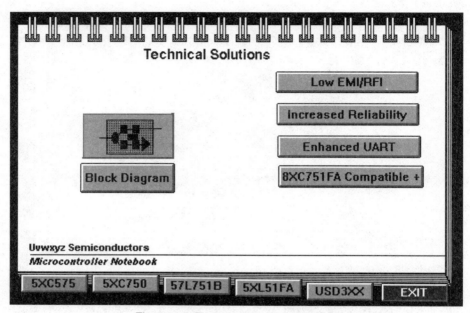

Figure 4.5 Technical section – top level.

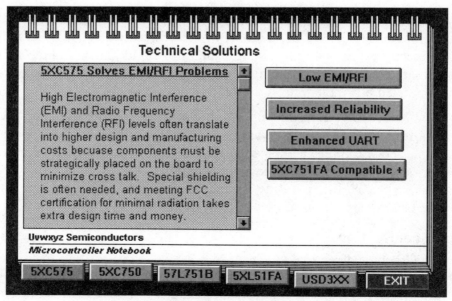

Figure 4.6 Scrolling text gives more detail.

When the user is finished exploring, he or she simply clicks the highlighted tab to return to home base. The user can also jump to any other component's home base by pressing its tab at the bottom of the notebook.

Additional Elements

In addition to the animation, buttons, and scrolling text windows shown here, I also used hypertext links embedded in the scrolling text that lead to more in-depth information.

The Importance of Color

Color is an extremely important part of your presentation. Unfortunately, I couldn't show its impact here. For example, the EXIT button is red with white text, and each of the tabs are different pastel colors. The background behind the notebook is a dark purple-red, and the notebook's cover is deep blue. Use color sparingly but creatively to make your point and add interest and excitement to your interactive presentations.

Drawing Your Map

Physically drawing your map on a piece of paper or on the computer's screen is the final step before you enter your presentation into the computer.

Some tools, such as the Apple Media Tool, allow you to create an interactive highway right on the screen while creating the presentation itself. If you are at all familiar with computerized project-management charts, then conceptualizing and creating a road map on-screen will be a snap. Regardless of which software package you use, you can always rely on good old paper and pencil. Begin by blocking in the primary destinations, then follow this by drawing interconnecting lines between them and a central home base. Once you've got the basics worked out you can expand each destination block and connect its elements.

Figure 4.7 shows a typical Apple Media Tool upper-level map to give you the idea.

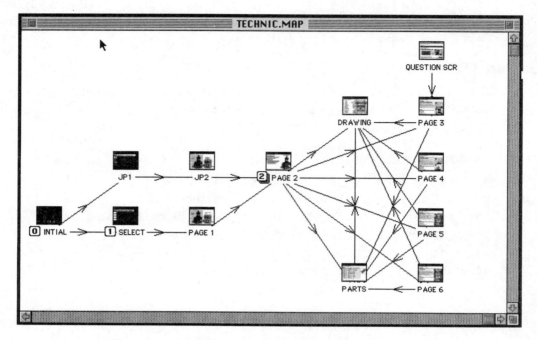

Figure 4.7 Upper-level presentation map – Apple Media Tool.

Buttons, Objects, and Hot Spots

You design your presentation so that once the user gets to a destination
screen, he or she can then explore to a further depth by pressing buttons,
objects, or hot spots on the computer's screen. As you've seen in my "Hot
Products" example, some programs provide ready-made buttons that you simply place on the screen. Depending on the authoring application you use, you
assign actions to a button, object, or hot spot by using either a scripting language or by selecting from an option list.

Astound, for example, lets you place buttons (or invisible buttons) or objects
anywhere on your screen. You can then assign the action that occurs when the
button, invisible area, or object is pushed by selecting from an easy-to-use
list, as shown in Fig. 4.8.

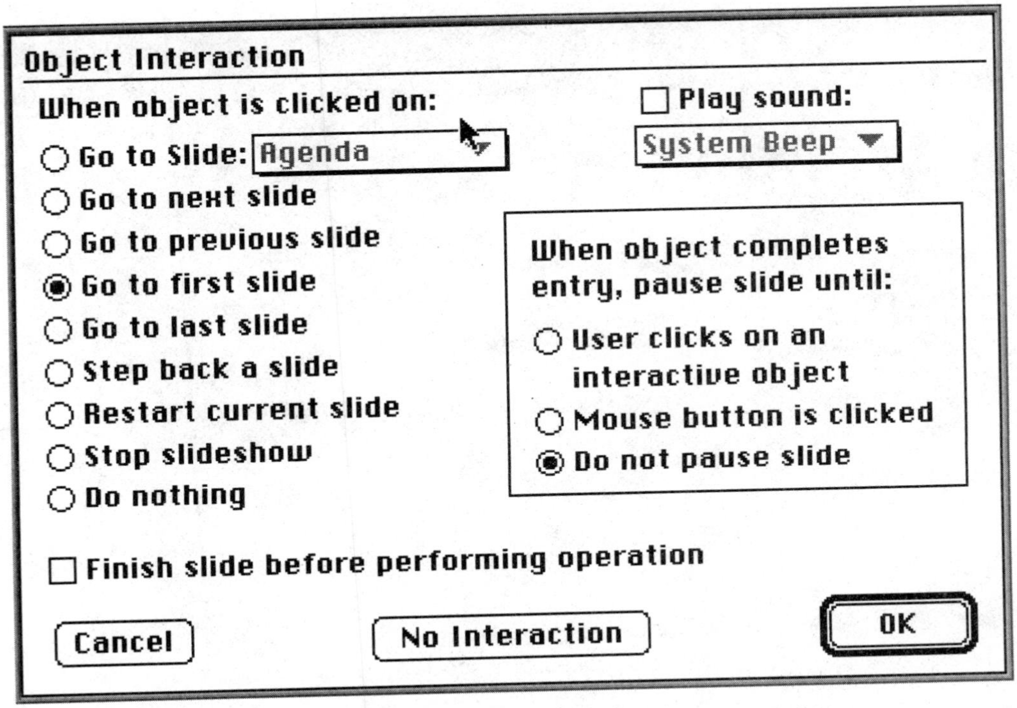

Object Interaction

When object is clicked on: ☐ **Play sound:**

○ Go to Slide: [Agenda ▾]   [System Beep ▾]
○ Go to next slide
○ Go to previous slide
◉ Go to first slide   When object completes
○ Go to last slide   entry, pause slide until:
○ Step back a slide
○ Restart current slide   ○ User clicks on an
○ Stop slideshow   interactive object
○ Do nothing   ○ Mouse button is clicked
                                             ◉ Do not pause slide

☐ Finish slide before performing operation

[Cancel]   [No Interaction]   [OK]

Figure 4.8 Defining an object's interaction - Astound!

Creating a Hot Spot

You can place an invisible object on the screen, over a picture, for example, to create an on-screen "hot spot." When the cursor is on the invisible hot spot and the mouse button is clicked, or when the cursor wipes over the invisible on-screen area, an interaction occurs. A good example of this is shown in one of *Apple Media Tool*'s tutorials, entitled Pharmaceuticals. This interactive presentation lets the user learn about one of many different antibiotics. This demonstration application is an excellent advanced use of interactive multimedia. Figure 4.9 shows part of the opening screen. When the user clicks on a photograph of a group of medicines (in this case the Seputal pills), he or she is taken to another screen for further exploration.

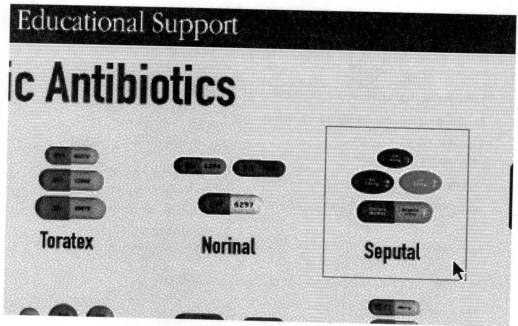

Figure 4.9 Hot spots – Apple Media Tool.

Video Considerations

Video can be a powerful addition to your interactive presentation. The only drawback today is that quite a bit of disk space is needed to store video information. This makes it almost impossible to put your presentation on a floppy disk for distribution to a wide audience. Also, to be able to play back video on a Macintosh computer, the end user must have the QuickTime application installed on a computer running System 7 software. Video drivers must be installed on a PC running Windows to be able to view the video.

Both Apple and Microsoft are working to overcome these drawbacks, so don't shy away from using this powerful medium. Whenever possible, include video in your interactive presentations. Chapter 9, "*Video*," gives you a good grounding for working with video and introduces you to software packages and video hardware.

Apple Media Tool's Pharmaceuticals interactive demonstration effectively uses a QuickTime movie of a doctor explaining the use and effectiveness of selected antibiotics, as shown in Fig. 4.10.

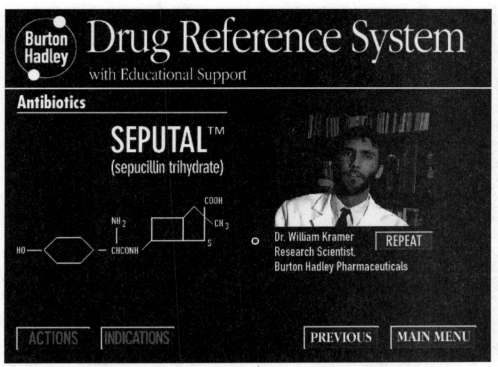

Figure 4.10 Doctor explains antibiotic use – Apple Media Tool.

Another, extremely effective, use of video in an interactive presentation is *Apple Media Tool*'s demonstration presentation entitled *"Technical."* The Technical presentation shows how to perform complex mechanical assembly, step by step (Fig. 4.11). This interactive presentation takes the place of an instructor and has added advantages:

- It can be distributed to an unlimited number of people.

- It can be viewed as many times as needed, allowing the assembler to work at his or her own pace.

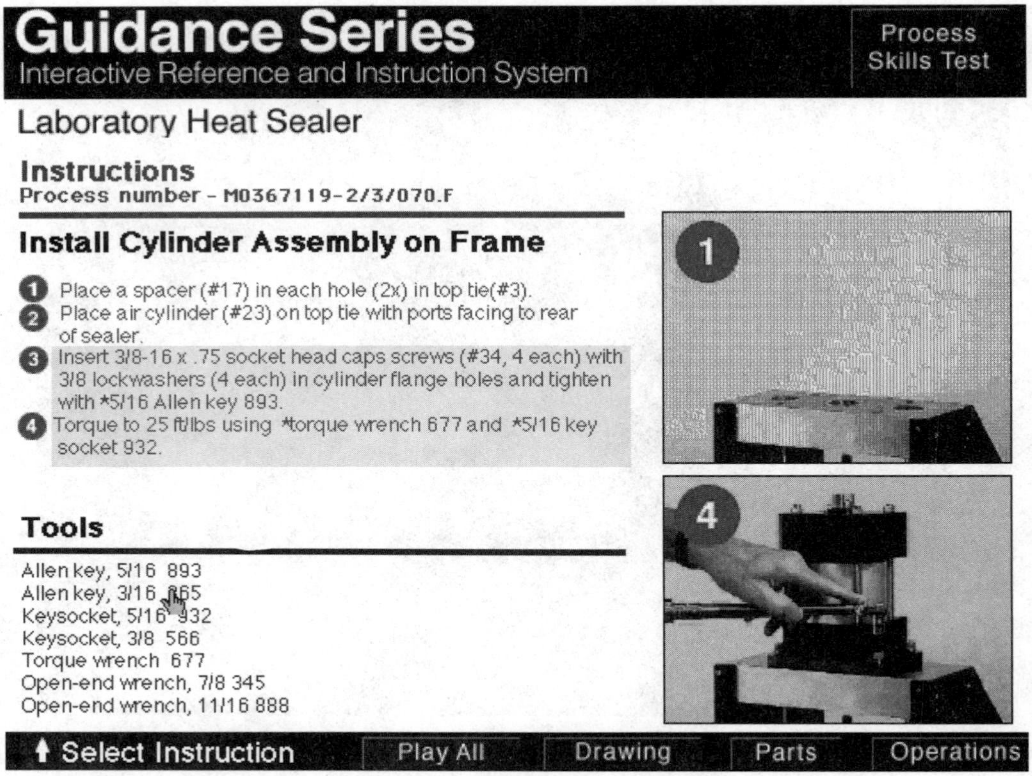

Guidance Series
Interactive Reference and Instruction System

Process
Skills Test

Laboratory Heat Sealer

Instructions
Process number – M0367119-2/3/070.F

Install Cylinder Assembly on Frame

1 Place a spacer (#17) in each hole (2x) in top tie(#3).

2 Place air cylinder (#23) on top tie with ports facing to rear of sealer.

3 Insert 3/8-16 x .75 socket head caps screws (#34, 4 each) with 3/8 lockwashers (4 each) in cylinder flange holes and tighten with *5/16 Allen key 893.

4 Torque to 25 ft/lbs using *torque wrench 677 and *5/16 key socket 932.

Tools

Allen key, 5/16 893
Allen key, 3/16 865
Keysocket, 5/16 932
Keysocket, 3/8 566
Torque wrench 677
Open-end wrench, 7/8 345
Open-end wrench, 11/16 888

↑ Select Instruction   Play All   Drawing   Parts   Operations

Figure 4.11 Interactive instructional video – Apple Media Tool.

Photographs Make the Point

Photographs can do more then just spice up your presentation. They can introduce your audience to people in your organization, show off your facilities, or could even be used by a real estate broker to give prospective buyers a simulated walk around a neighborhood or a house tour. The *Apple Media Tool* Training demonstration application shows photographs of each component of the assembly. When the user highlights a listed component, its photograph is displayed in the box to the right, as shown in Fig. 4.12.

Guidance Series
Interactive Reference and Instruction System

Laboratory Heat Sealer

Parts

PART NUMBER	QTY	OPERATION	DESCRIPTION
108	4	Clamp Strip	Retainer
2345890-1	4	Socket Head Cap	Screw 3/8-16x.75
2334578-3	8	Socket Head Cap	Screw 10-24x.75
2448913-8	4	Spring	Clamp hold off
2345890-1	1	Lock Washer	Washer
2334578-3	1	Lock Washer 3/8	Washer
2448913-8	4	Upper Spring Rings	Retainer
2353007-2	1	Lower Spring Ring	Retainer
2345890-1	1	Socket Head Bolt	1/2-20x1
2334578-3	2	Flow Control	Valve
2448913-8	2	Spacer Ring	Spacer
2353007-2	1	Elbow Fitting	Fitting
2345890-1	2	Reducer	Fitting
2334578-3	1	Cylinder Assm.	Cylinder
2448913-8	1	Dieplate - Lower	Die
2448445-8	1	Dieplate - Upper	Die

Figure 4.12 Using instructional photographs – Apple Media Tool.

Adding Photographs

You can add photographs to your presentations in one of three ways:

- Buy digitized stock photographs and import them into your presentation.

- Scan your photographs into your presentation using a color scanner.

- Have your photographs put on a Kodak Photo CD, and then import them into your presentation from your CD-ROM.

If you are going to do a lot of work with photographs you should purchase a tool like *Adobe Photoshop* for the Macintosh or Windows. *Adobe Photoshop* allows you to retouch your photographs and add special effects to give your presentation a polished, professional look. The power available to manipulate digitized photographs is truly amazing. *Photoshop*, coupled with third-party extensions like *Kai's Power Tools*, lets you create the same effects you see in the slickest advertisements. Look into these tools. They are well worth the investment.

Timing, Storyboards, and Scripts

A storyboard, as used in the movie industry, consists of a sequential series of sketches that show how the action flows in each scene. The director uses these sketches as a road map during production. Creating a detailed visual storyboard for your presentation is always a good idea. It keeps the project focused and on track. In addition to a visual storyboard, you should also prepare a written storyboard that includes timing information, narrative script, and accompanying action for sequences that run automatically.

For example, when the user gets to a specific slide and requests specific information by pressing an on-screen button, a movie might start with narrated voice-over accompanied by bulleted text that appears on the screen. Coordinating all this action takes planning. In this section we'll review part of a storyboard that I worked on for a high-tech company. In designing this presentation we developed a script that was then broken down into short chunks of information, or frames, and timed to work with the action.

Before looking at the script, you should know that most interactive authoring software packages include timing tools that let you coordinate events as shown in the *Astound* screen shot in Fig. 4.13.

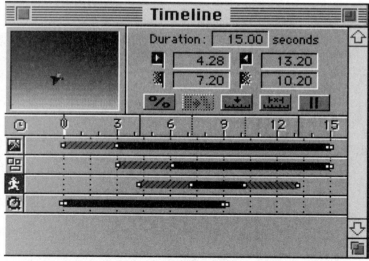

Figure 4.13 Coordinating and timing events in Astound.

However, before you can use tools like these effectively you have to have a plan – and that plan is formalized on a storyboard worksheet.

The Storyboard Worksheet

The following example storyboard worksheet includes the introduction and part of the corporate overview sections of a much larger piece. The entire interactive presentation introduces a set of engineering software tools, shows how they operate, and presents corporate background information. We just show a portion of it in Table 4.2 to show you how to lay out and work with a storyboard worksheet.

Use the format in Table 4.2 as a template to help you develop your presentation.

TABLE 4.2   Storyboard Worksheet Example

Frame	Voice-over	Action
Introduction		
Intro 1 14.2 secs	It's a tough world out there. Today's design engineers are under tremendous pressure. They've got to handle short product life cycles, increased design complexity, and reduced product cost while increasing product quality.	Music Animated walls representing pressures being exerted on a wire-frame figure who finds solutions to pressures with Phoenix II. • Short product life cycles • Increased design complexity • Reduced product cost

TABLE 4.2 Storyboard Worksheet Example

Frame	Voice-over	Action
Intro 2 29.36 secs	Phoenix II meets these challenges with a suite of integrated EDA tools that: • Have an open, flexible framework • Are tightly integrated with other vendors' tools • Support CFI and other industry standards • Support popular methodologies, simulators, and layout tools	Corporate logo lands on walls and breaks them up. Bulleted text of advantages in sync to narration – basically the same as script, but more concise.
Intro 3 32.3 secs	This presentation takes you on a self-guided tour of Phoenix as it works with a complex computer peripheral design, from concept to implementation. You'll see how Phoenix II is used from Design Entry to Analysis to Synthesis to Test and, finally, to PCB layout. The resultant board includes an array of FPGAs, PLDs, ASICS, and analog components. Select a topic and take a short guided tour through each stage of the design process.	Transition to main menu.

TABLE 4.2   Storyboard Worksheet Example

Frame	Voice-over	Action
About Phoenix Corporation (Corporate Overview)		
CO1 16.2 secs	Phoenix Corporation was founded in 1983, and is one of today's fastest-growing EDA vendors. Phoenix worldwide organization, with 1992 sales in excess of $65 million, has a long and consistent record of steady growth and profitability.	Show animated growth chart.
CO2 15 secs	With the addition of X Systems, a leader in high-performance VHDL simulation, and Y Design, the leader in timing analysis and signal integrity, Phoenix offers an unmatched set of advanced EDA tools.	• Advanced EDA tools • X Systems • Y Design

Adding Narration

To add narration to your presentation:

1. Block out the narration with its relationship to other effects and action on your storyboard worksheet.
2. Read the script and time it using a stopwatch. Accurately record the time it takes for the computerized frame to do its build.
3. Write the longest of the two times in the worksheet's *Frame* column.
4. Have a professional narrator record the script within the total frame time. (Have the narrator identify each frame, then pause before continuing on to the next frame.)

Input the recorded narration into your computer. Then electronically edit it and add it to your presentation. (*See Chap. 8, "Sound," to learn how to input and manipulate digital sound.*)

To add narration and audio effects to most applications you edit and prepare the sounds in a separate audio editor and then import them into your application. *Astound* is one exception to this rule. It includes a built-in audio editor that is fine for adding simple narration and sound effects to each frame (Fig. 4-14).

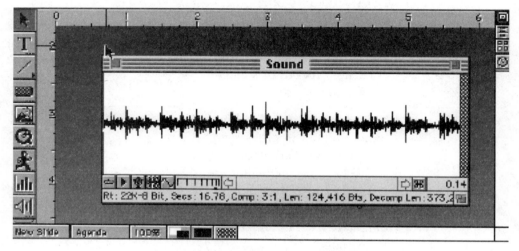

Figure 4.14   Astound's built-in audio editor.

Interactive Tool Tour

Let's take a brief tour of some of the tools you can use to create your interactive presentations. These overviews preview some of today's premier authoring tools so you can become familiar with their inner workings and capabilities. All these software packages are evolving rapidly, with new features and capabilities being added constantly. The overviews focus on each package's underlying structure and strengths to help you decide which tool fits your authoring style. Review Table 4.1 before beginning the tour.

Authorware Preview

Name: **ACTION!**

Manufacturer: Macromedia

Authoring: Macintosh & Windows

Playback: Macintosh & Windows

Tool Level: I

Action!, by Macromedia, has all the bells and whistles you need to create effective interactive presentations. It is <u>not</u>, however, related in capability or implementation to Macromedia's premier authoring tool, Director. Action! uses the excellent animations created in Director, but is its own animal, with its own unique way of allowing you to design live presentations or create self-running demos for your next trade show.

Scenes, Objects, and Things That Go *Bump*!

Action!'s presentations are made of scenes that are like slides in other presentation packages, with the added dimension of time. Each scene contains objects (such as text, graphics, and sounds) that you draw using the provided tool set, import from other applications, or import from the ClipMedia™ library supplied with Action!

Adding Charts, Motion, Sound, and Interactivity

Most of Action!'s Tool Palette tools – pointer, text tool, circle, and polygons – look, act, and are used just like their counterparts in drawing programs. But here the similarity ends. Four unique Action! tools, <u>chart</u>, <u>action</u>, <u>sound</u>, and <u>link</u>, let you add charts, motion, sound, and interactivity to Action! presentations (Fig. 4.15).

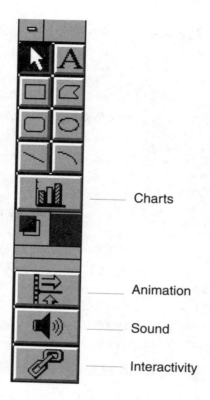

Figure 4.15   Four unique tools.

Charts

You use the chart tool on the Tool Palette to create charts by entering data directly or pasting data from other applications. You then plot the data in a format that best meets your needs. Charts styles are not Action!'s strongest point. You don't have a wide range of chart options to choose from, but what you do get is fine for most business applications. Action! also gives you the ability to animate the chart's individual components for added presentation impact (Fig. 4.16).

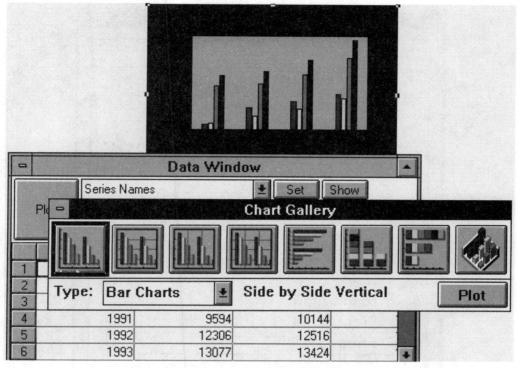

Figure 4.16   Animated charts.

For example, bars representing several quarters' sales figures can glide into and out of your presentation one quarter at a time. This animated action highlights sales trends and gives you time to make comments or include timed voice-over while your presentation runs.

Motion

You can apply motion to any object in a scene. You use the motion tool to define the direction the object moves as it enters or leaves the scene, and apply transitions and light effects that affect the object's appearance (Fig. 4.17).

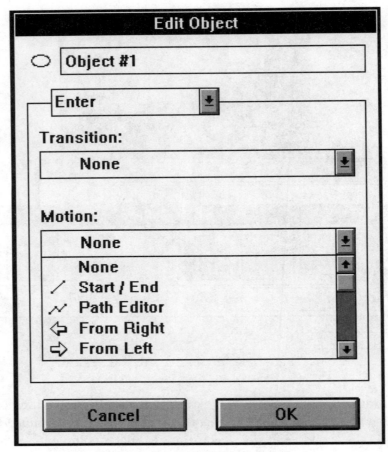

Figure 4.17   Applying action to Action!

For example, each line of bulleted text might fly onto the screen from the right. Then, when all the bullets are on the screen, the text could slowly dissolve, making an effective transition to the next scene. You can also grow charts and add sparkle to your animations and, for added effects, you can import an animation created in Director and use it as an object in your scene. The included ClipMedia file contains several ready-to-use Director animations.

Sound

Action!'s sound tool lets you apply sound to any object in your presentation. The sound, including voice-overs, can play when the object is visible on the screen or as background with no linkage to objects.

Action! lets you use digitized sound stored on disk, or sound from an audio CD-ROM attached to your computer. The ClipMedia file contains a number of sound effects and musical numbers ready to incorporate into your presentation.

Interactivity

Action! presentations can be interactive, allowing the viewer to control the flow of the presentation by clicking on-screen buttons. You use the link tool in the Tool Palette to turn any object in a scene into a button, or you can create a new button from scratch. Each button has an associated action that takes you to a different location in the presentation. For example, each bullet in a product list could be a button. As you discuss each item, you click the bullet to go to a scene that describes the product in detail; then, when you're finished, press another button to return to the main menu.

Timing Is Everything

As you create objects in a scene, they appear in the presentation window and in the Timeline window that shows how all objects in a scene relate to one another (Fig. 4.18). Each object in the Timeline appears as a bar; the length of a bar shows the duration of the object in the current scene. You stretch or shrink an object's bar in the Timeline to increase or decrease the object's on-screen duration or to move the object to a different time in the scene.

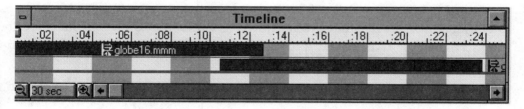

Figure 4.18   Timeline.

Tutorials and Documentation

Action! comes with a well-illustrated *User's Guide,* Help files, and a sample presentation that shows off its chart-building animation and lets you interactively explore its sound, motion, and interactivity capabilities.

Authorware Preview

Name:	**Animation Works Interactive**
Manufacturer:	Gold Disk
Authoring:	Windows
Playback:	Windows
Tool Level:	I

Animation Works Interactive's strong suit is, as its name implies, animation. It is, however, a full-feature interactive presentation tool that you can use to create and integrate all the familiar multimedia elements: sound, video, animation, and more.

Creating Animation Works Movies

Animation Works has two primary work spaces: the Cell Editor and Movie Editor. You create, edit, and test animated movies in the Cell Editor using traditional overlay techniques and a wide assortment of drawing tools. You then use the animations in your presentation, which you create in the Movie Editor.

Animations created in the Cell Editor can also be used in Gold Disk's companion program, *Astound*.

Animation Works provides you with an optional electronic "onionskin" that you turn on to display a faint image of the previous or next cell. By comparing the changes from one image to another, you can draw accurate and realistic animations (Fig. 4.19).

A full library of ready-to-use animated "actors" is provided that you can use immediately in your presentations.

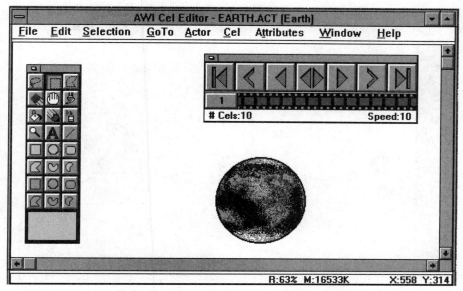

Figure 4.19   Cell Editor- Animation Works Interactive.

The Movie Editor

The Movie Editor screen (Fig. 4.20) is where you put all the elements of your presentation together. This work space contains an animation path menu bar, tape-player-type controls, and the animation(s) you've created in the Cell Editor.

You can import AVI video (and other formats, provided you have the correct driver), record sound directly from within the window, and create interactive elements that allow the user to control the action and direction of your presentation.

You can also "program" your presentation to control external Windows MCI devices, such as CD-ROMs and videodisc players. You key these events into exactly the right portion of your presentation to add sound, video, or other external actions.

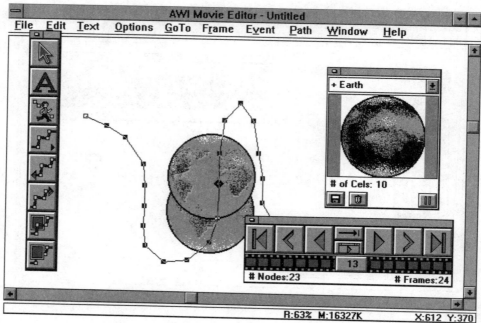

Figure 4.20   Movie Editor-Animation Works Interactive.

Interactivity

Scripting is not needed to create powerful interactivity with Animation Works Interactive. Any item or "actor" (an animated object) can be a button that controls where the presentation branches and what it displays or does (Fig. 4.21).

A button can also execute MCI commands for controlling devices like video hardware. Or a button could execute other programs or play other Animation Works Interactive files.

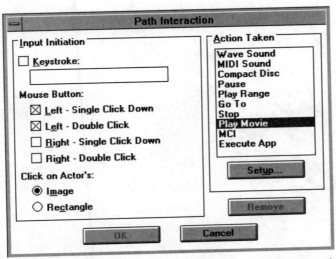

Figure 4.21   Path interactive set-up-Animation Works Interactive.

Tutorials and Documentation

Animation Works Interactive's documentation consists of a short *Getting Started* manual that tracks a software tutorial, and a *Reference* guide. Although all the information you need is included, you have to do some hunting and pecking to find it. There is no user's manual and going through the tutorial is a must if you want to use it for more than animation creation.

Authorware Preview

Name: **The Apple Media Kit:**
                         Apple Media Tool
                         & Programming Environment

Manufacturer: Apple Computer

Authoring: Apple Macintosh

Playback: Macintosh and Windows

The Apple Media Kit consists of two components (Apple Media Tool and the Apple Media Tool Programming Environment) that are used solo or in concert to produce media-rich projects for both Macintosh and Windows platforms.

TheApple Media Tool is a level I interactive multimedia authoring tool - no scripting is required to produce high-quality presentations that can be played on both Macintosh and Windows computers.

In cases where additional levels of interactivity are required, you can save your project as a text program and bring it into the Apple Media Tool Programming Environment for further enhancement (if you purchase this extra tool). Programming professionals use the Apple Media Language (a new general-purpose, object-oriented programming language influenced by Pascal and Eiffel) to achieve enhancements such as:

- Apple's speech technology

- High-performance sprite animations

- A database search engine for an electronic catalog that can be accessed across a network

Developing a Project with Apple Media Tool

You begin your design work in the Apple Media Tool in the Map window. This is where you create a visual map representation of your project. In this window you point and click your mouse button to create paths between screens and name screens, assemble and assign media to screens and more. Figure 4.22 shows a typical Map window with paths between screens and media elements listed in media list miniwindows. Media elements can be PICT images, QuickTime movies, sound (in AIFF or WAVE formats), or editable and noneditable text.

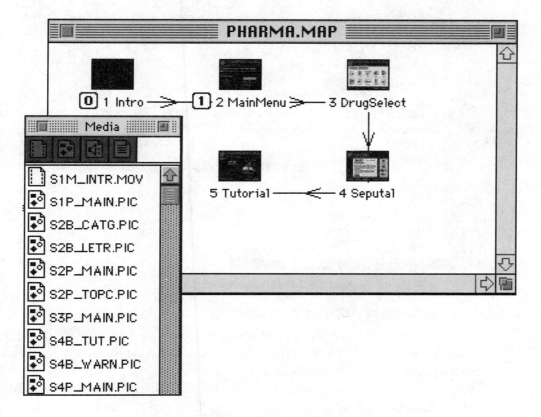

Figure 4.22   Map window-Apple Media Tool.

The Screen Window

Clicking on a screen element in the Map window opens that screen and displays its objects. Once the Screen window is open, you can create new objects and fill them with media content from the media elements listed in the Media miniwindows, or you can work with existing objects (Fig. 4.23).

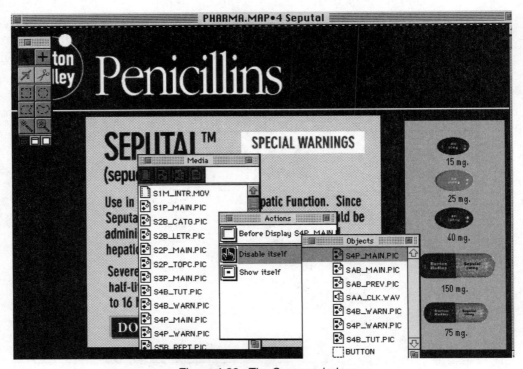

Figure 4.23 The Screen window.

Controlling Objects and Adding Interactivity

You can control the length of time an object remains on the screen and make it into a hot region that is sensitive to mouse activity. An Actions miniwindow displays actions that you can assign to buttons and hot objects. In addition, there is an event pop-up menu that allows you to select from the eight different kinds of event objects the Apple Media Tool can respond to.

Fourteen different command actions that an object executes in response to a particular event are listed in a Command Action pop-up menu. To round out the possibilities, Apple Media Tool also includes a wide selection of special between-slide effects and point-and-click linking to other elements in your presentation.

The combination of all this easy-to-use and well-thought-out power results in fast and efficient multimedia presentation development. In fact, this tool is the only tool that lends itself specifically to team development, for even more efficiency.

We found that the basic Media Tool was just perfect for creating almost any interactive business presentation. The Apple Media Tool and its companion, Programming Environment, are sold separately, and you may want to get your feet wet with the basic tool before considering the higher-level tool.

The Programming Environment is designed for advanced programmers. The documentation is written in "engineereze," but the production results are stunning - after a lot of time and effort.

Tutorials and Documentation

The Apple Media Tool comes with a CD-ROM that includes three inventive and creative demonstration interactive presentations. One of these, a walking tour of San Francisco, is used as an effective tutorial with the accompanying *Getting Started* book. The *User's Guide* is short and to the point, and this, coupled with the excellent examples, can quickly help get you on your way to producing your own high-quality interactive presentations.

Authorware Preview

Name:	**Astound**
Manufacturer:	Gold Disk
Authoring:	Macintosh & Windows
Playback:	Macintosh & Windows
Tool Level:	I

Astound, by Gold Disk, is a multipurpose, almost all-inclusive, multimedia presentation creation tool. It has all the functionality of base presentation software, such as PowerPoint and Aldus Persuasion, plus adds advanced animation, sound, timing, and interactive capabilities so you can create a business presentation at virtually any level, for almost any audience.

Easy to Produce Overheads

Astound has all the functionality you need to create color or black-and-white overheads or slides, complete with outline, speaker notes, and handouts. When producing basic presentations, the learning curve is virtually nonexistent. The interface is extremely intuitive and easy to work with.

Basic Computerized Slide Shows

Creating computerized slide shows with text bullets that build on the screen and with fancy transitions between slides is astoundingly easy in Astound. You can choose from a list of effects and watch how they work in a preview window before applying them to your presentation as shown in Fig. 4.24.

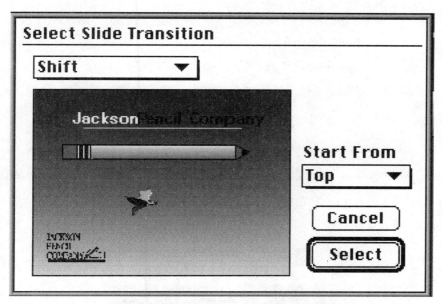

Figure 4.24 Slide transition effects—Astound.

Adding Animation and Video

Astound comes with an animation library full of objects, people, and animals called *actors* you use in your presentations to add action. It also lets you assign special transitions and motion effects to any object and define its path and movement about the screen.

Charts and graphs also come alive with animated action in Astound. You create three-dimensional full-color charts in a familiar spreadsheet window, then easily add customized animation to each of the chart's elements.

You can place and edit QuickTime movies in the Macintosh version, and add PIC animations. QuickTime movies created in the Macintosh can be distributed for playback under Windows. You can also edit and place Window-compatible movies and animations in Astound's Window version (Fig. 4.25).

The video editor allows you to:

- Scale the size of the movie

- Scroll or step through the movie

- Cause a movie to loop

- Adjust the sound level

- Adjust the rate of play

- Cut, copy, and paste portions of movies to create a composite

- Set markers in QuickTime movies

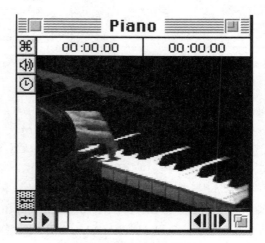

Figure 4.25 Editing video.

Adding Sound

Using Astound's built-in sound editor, you can add narration and sound effects while watching a slide build on screen. On the Macintosh, Astound supports the built-in microphone and Macromind's *MacRecorder*, and on the PC it supports most popular sound file editors.

Timing Events

With so much happening - sound, animation, video, animated graphs and charts, text builds, and transitions - you've got to coordinate events. Many events occur at the same time, or overlap, and an easy-to-use timeline editor is a must. Astound's Timeline editor makes it easy to coordinate all this action

(Fig. 4.26). You double-click on an object or an event button and it appears in the window of the Timeline editor. You then use your mouse to move its timeline in relation to the other events in the editor.

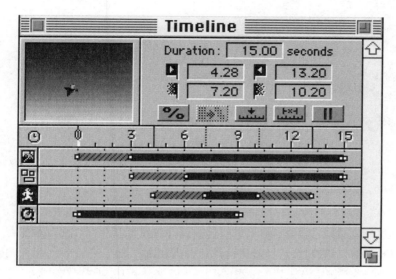

Figure 4.26 Astound's Timeline editor.

Interactivity

You add interactivity by placing buttons anywhere to play sounds, go to other slides, restart presentations, and more. The buttons can be customized, and interactivity can be assigned to any object in the presentation.

Tutorials and Documentation

Astound's documentation is first-class, and covers all you need to know to take advantage of all its many features. The software also ships with an eight-step tutorial that shows off all the tool's capabilities, from basic slide production to full animation with video, sound, and a bevy of effects.

Authorware Preview

Name:	**COMPEL**
Manufacturer:	Asymetrix
Authoring:	Windows
Playback:	Windows
Tool Level:	I

COMPEL, by Asymetrix, has the features, power, and ease-of-use that make it ideal for creating and playing standard and interactive presentations on Windows-equipped personal computers. Its interactive features include pre-fab buttons, hot words, special event triggering, and hyperlinking - and it adds zap with special effects for bulleted text and slide transitions. Its multimedia capabilities allow you to link sound effects and video directly to on-screen actions, making it easy to quickly produce full-fledged interactive multimedia presentations for virtually any application.

Essentially, COMPEL is the level I version of Aysemtrix's *Multimedia Tool-Book*. No scripting is needed with COMPEL to create interactive slides, and all its advanced features are accessed easily from within its well-thought-out graphical user interface.

Starting with the Basics

COMPEL has all the basic business presentation capabilities you need to produce anything from standard overhead transparencies to full-fledged interactive multimedia presentations. You can quickly and easily produce all these presentation basics in a friendly and easy-to-use work space (complete with context-sensitive messages to guide you) (Fig. 4.27):

- 35mm slides

- Full-color or black-and-white transparencies

- Audience handouts

- Speaker notes

- Basic computerized on-screen presentations with simple bulleted text builds, special effects, and transitions

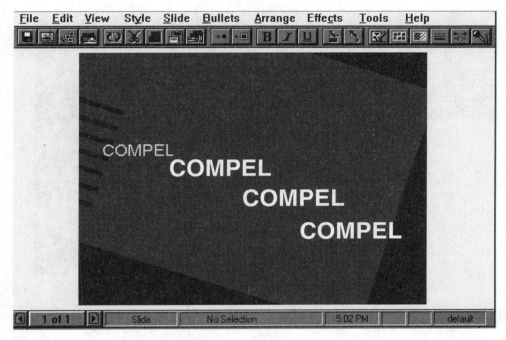

Figure 4.27 Intuitive and easy-to-use work space—COMPEL.

Charts and Graphs Make the Point

COMPEL's built-in chart editor is set up just like a familiar spreadsheet application. In it you store, organize, and manipulate your data to create effective and attractive charts. You can also import data directly from popular spreadsheet programs for chart creation, or export it to other applications for further manipulation (Fig. 4.28).

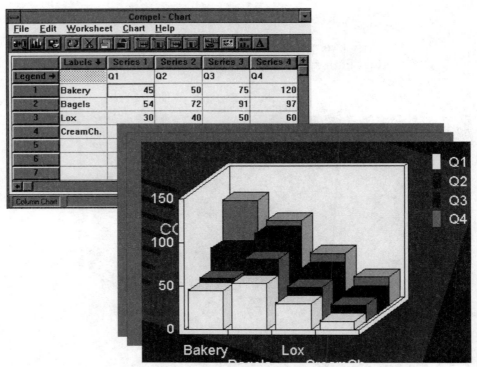

Figure 4.28 Creating professional-quality charts and graphs.

Adding Animation

COMPEL comes with an animation clip-art library full of objects, people, and animals you use in your presentations to add action. It also lets you animate any on-screen object by:

5. Dragging it to a starting position
6. Dragging it to an ending position
7. Clicking OK

Once you've defined the object's motion path, you adjust a slider to set its speed, and finally link it to an event- or user-initiated action.

Multimedia Power

You can add the impact of multimedia to your COMPEL presentations by combining text and graphics with sound, video, or animation. COMPEL lets you work from two sources of multimedia:

1. Multimedia stored on your computer's hard disk, CD-ROM, or floppy disk. For example, if you have audio hardware installed on your computer, you can use COMPEL to play sounds stored in a wave audio (.WAV) file on your hard disk.

2. Multimedia information that resides on separate hardware, like an external CD audio player, a videodisc, and other media devices that store sound and video.

COMPEL has the built-in flexibility to control a variety of media files and devices using Windows 3.1 MCI, a standard control interface for multimedia. COMPEL uses this MCI standard so you can easily combine sound and images in your presentation, and play media files created in other software tools that comply with the MCI standard. For example, you can include animation created in any MCI-compatible software package in your COMPEL presentations.

MediaBlitz!

COMPEL ships with a group of companion programs called *MediaBlitz* that make it easy for you to compile combinations of sound, graphics, video, and animation clips (a *clip* refers to a portion of a media file) along a timeline to create a synchronized multimedia event that COMPEL calls a *score*.

You create scores in MediaBlitz's *ScoreMaker* window using sound (CD audio, wave audio, and MIDI sound), bit-map graphics, digital video, and animation (Fig. 4.29). You then integrate your score into your application using MediaBlitz's *ScorePlayer* application.

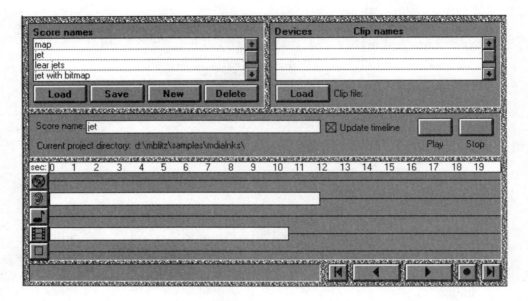

Figure 4.29 ScoreMaker window—COMPEL/MediaBlitz.

Interactivity

Selecting the button tool from COMPEL's handy tool palette, lets you create a button as large as the whole slide or as small as two pixels. You can set the button's label, describe its appearance from <u>invisible</u> to <u>standard push-button,</u> and define the action that occurs when it is pressed or passed over by the mouse cursor.

Instead of scattering buttons on a slide for all interactive actions, COMPEL allows you to create hot words that trigger a hyperlink or media link to other areas of the slide or to invoke media.

These two features help make COMPEL a good candidate for most of your interactive presentation needs.

Tutorials and Documentation

COMPEL ships on disk and with a CD-ROM that includes demonstrations and tutorials that give you an overview of the tool's capabilities and quickly get you started creating your own interactive presentations. The manual is well written and organized and covers everything you need to know to take advantage of this easy-to-use production and presentation tool.

Authorware Preview

Name: **Director**

Manufacturer: Macromedia

Authoring: Macintosh and Windows

Playback: Macintosh & Windows

Tool Level: II

Director, by Macromedia, is a powerful authoring and presentation tool that includes three sections allowing you to create interactive applications with or without using their Lingo scripting language.

- <u>Studio</u>. You create graphics and complex animation in the Studio environment for use in the Overview window and Interactive sections.

- <u>Overview</u>. The Overview window is a complete authoring environment that allows you to create complex interactive presentations without using their scripting language.

- <u>Interactivity</u>. The Interactive section includes all the power of the Overview section with the added flexibility of Lingo, Director's scripting language.

As one of the first multimedia production tools, Director has set the standard for those that followed. It has evolved to become the choice of many of today's multimedia business users and CD-title producers.

Director's Overview Window

Director's Overview window is where you construct your presentation (Fig. 4.30). This versatile work space allows you to import graphics, such as Mac-Paint and PICT-formatted documents, Director movies, accelerated movies, and sound. It also lets you drop in timing transitions, create effects between "slides," and add motion to bulleted text.

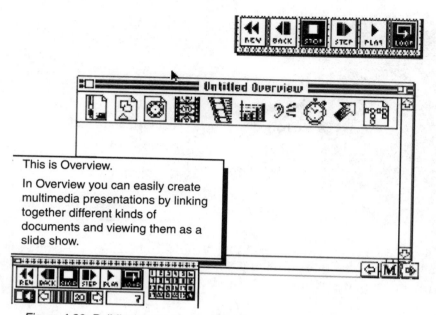

Figure 4.30 Building an interactive application in Director's Overview window.

The setting is very intuitive. You move and connect icon representations of each function in their order of appearance, and then use tape-player-type controls to review your masterpiece. During your production you bounce in and out of Director's Studio, where you create dazzling animations and graphic effects (Fig. 4.31).

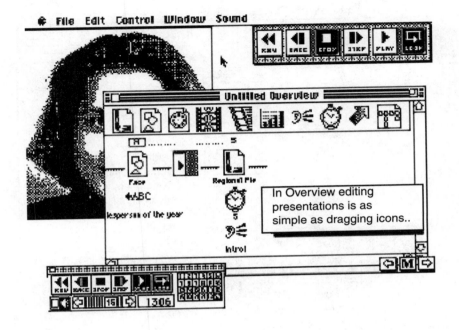

Figure 4.31   Overview's intuitive icon building blocks.

Director's Studio

The Studio allows you to create complex animations with multiple objects (called *cast members*) and accurately time multiple events for that professional touch. Figure 4.32 shows a Director score, including a number of precisely timed events that you craft one step at a time while monitoring and adjusting each element of your presentation.

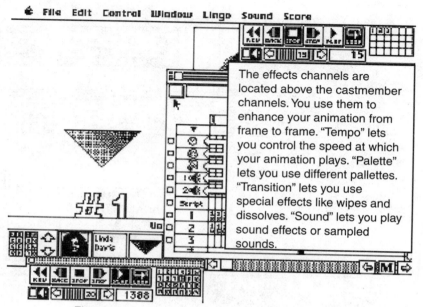

The effects channels are located above the castmember channels. You use them to enhance your animation from frame to frame. "Tempo" lets you control the speed at which your animation plays. "Palette" lets you use different pallettes. "Transition" lets you use special effects like wipes and dissolves. "Sound" lets you play sound effects or sampled sounds.

Figure 4.32   Studio's score — precise event timing.

The Studio is much more than an animation maker and organizer. It is also a sophisticated artist's workshop. You can bring a "cast member" into the studio for a quick color touch-up, create inked masks and matting, manipulate QuickDraw and bit-mapped text, perform complex drawing tasks, work with 32-bit images, and more.

Enhanced interaction with Lingo

Once you've developed your basic presentation and its elements in Overview and Studio, you can present it as is or move on to Director's powerful suite of interactive tools and Lingo scripting language. Director's interactive power is greatly enhanced by the power of Lingo (Fig. 4.33).

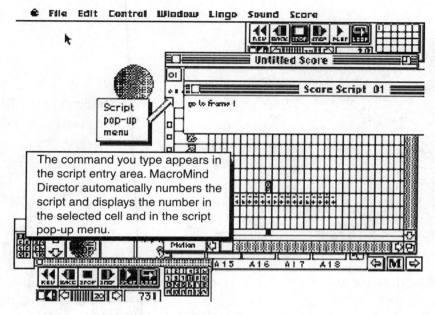

Figure 4.33   Interactive Lingo programming.

A Lingo script is a set of instructions that tell Director to perform specific tasks while a Director movie is running. A typical script contains one or more Lingo statements. These statements are single lines of code, written in an easy-to-learn English-like language. For example, "go to frame 1" simply means what it says! Most of Lingo is like this.

Tutorials and Documentation

Director comes with excellent documentation and tutorials to get you up and running in short order. The software comes with an interactive guided tour - produced using Director, of course - that walks you through the Overview window, into the Studio, and includes basic interactive techniques.

Authorware Preview

Name:	**Multimedia ToolBook**
Manufacturer:	Asymetrix
Authoring:	Windows
Playback:	Windows
Tool Level:	II

Multimedia ToolBook, by Asymetrix, is a multifaceted multimedia production tool that can be used to develop anything from an interactive business presentation or multimedia title to a full-fledged Microsoft Windows application.

This software construction kit comes with its own extensive scripting language, OpenScript, that lets advanced users develop virtually <u>any</u> Windows application they can think of — from simple device controllers to complex spreadsheets, time management software, and even multimedia authoring and presentation tools like COMPEL.

Even though ToolBook packs a lot of power, it comes with an extensive package of templates that make it relatively easy to become productive fast. The provided library includes fully developed applications, complete with guided tours that let you go behind the scenes to learn how each application is constructed.

The library also includes a complete catalog of useful scripts that let you control everything from color to navigation to screen layout. You first learn what each script does, copy it to the clipboard, then paste it into your in-progress project.

Building a Book

You build applications and multimedia presentations as if you are building a book. You add pages to the book, then use ToolBook's hypertext ability to navigate from page to page and from object to object within each page.

Scripting language knowledge is not needed to get started. ToolBook includes animations, buttons, and tons of other already developed pieces you simply cut and paste into your application.

Slide Show Builder

A Slide Show Builder is another of the many tools available from the library (Fig. 4.34). The Slide Show Builder provides you with an easy way to make interactive, on-line presentations with ToolBook. This program creates new books based on the template style and color combination that you choose. Then, all you have to do is type text into each page of your new book. Once you finish building a slide show book, you simply run it and begin your show.

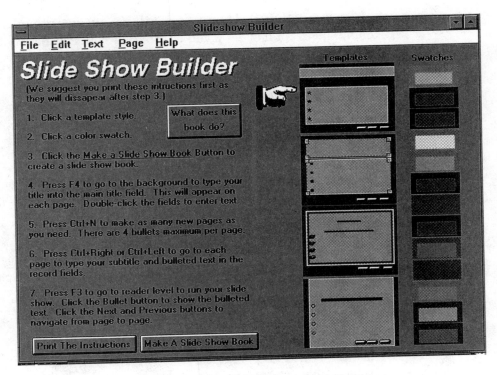

Figure 4.34   ToolBook's Slide Show Builder.

Sample Applications and On-Line Tutorials

The sample applications provided with ToolBook illustrate different kinds of ToolBook applications. You can use them as a source of ideas, and for script and objects for your own applications. Most of the sample applications include a button or special command on the Help menu that explains how the application works, and each application's scripts include comments to make it easy for you to understand and apply them to your own needs. ToolBook's sample applications include the following:

- **Animation Primer** demonstrates animation creation techniques with examples you can use in your applications.

- **Bookshelf** lets you organize and launch ToolBook Applications with drag-and-drop icons.

- **Calculator** simulates a conventional calculator and provides functions to calculate loan payments.

- **Software Catalog and Data Validation Routines** provide sample pages for a catalog and a form that validates data entry (Fig. 4.35).

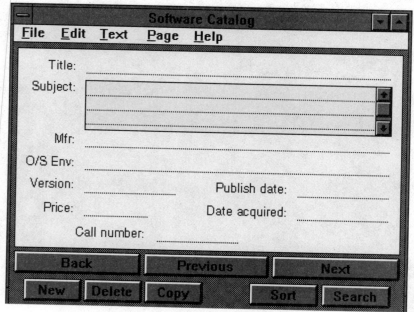

Figure 4.35 Software Catalog application.

- **Clip Art** is an extensive collection of art created from ToolBook draw objects that you can copy and paste into your books.

- **DayBook** is a graphical personal organizer for scheduling days, weeks, and months. It also allows the user to manage to-do lists and track contacts.

- **ToolBook dBASE/Exchange and dBASE Reader** allows you to import and export dBase files or build a browser book for viewing and updating dBase records while working in ToolBook.

- **Using Dynamic DataExchange** explains Dynamic Data Exchange (DDE) for ToolBook, and shows a "live" connection between ToolBook and Microsoft Excel.

- **Hypermedia Book** presents examples of hypermedia and hypertext for the PC, using buttons, hot words, and objects for navigation.

- **Scripts Notebook** provides special-purpose scripts and some advanced programming aids for ToolBook authors.

- **Slide Show Builder** provides templates that allow you to create on-line presentations.

- **ToolBook Speed Tips** demonstrates image drawing control and speed tricks.

- **Taquin** is a familiar game that uses scripts for positioning drag-and-drop objects in relation to each other.

Multimedia Buttons and Widgets

Controlling an external CD player, tape deck, or video player is easy with ToolBook's prewritten and configured interface buttons. *Multimedia Tour Book* and *Multimedia Widgets* are ToolBook applications that show you how to read wave audio, use bit-map graphics, control videodisc and CD audio players, use MIDI, take advantage of animation, and time events. Then, they let you choose from a wide selection of predesigned elements and use them directly in your ToolBook application. Multimedia ToolBook makes designing an interactive application slick and easy.

The controls in Fig. 4.36 are representative of the many controls and ready-to-use applications available in the Multimedia Widgets application. The controls shown let you select a clip from a CD and create a wave file from the clip. Complete instructions for using each page in Widget book are listed in a scrolling text window to the right of the buttons and sliders.

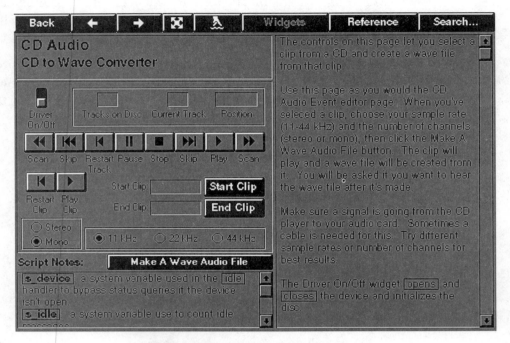

Figure 4.36   Multimedia Widgets example.

Interactive Training and Documentation

Multimedia ToolBook is for serious developers, and its documentation and interactive training cover all the bases.

ToolBook's hands-on training applications acquaint you with its features and teach you, step by step, how to use the OpenScript programming language.

- A Quick Tour program delivers a short interactive tour of ToolBook's features.

- An OpenScript Workbook is an on-line introduction to the OpenScript language.

These interactive tools, coupled with a complete example library and comprehensive <u>User's Guide</u> and <u>OpenScript Manual</u>, make this one of the best-documented tools on the market.

Be Still, My Beating Heart

The moment of truth has arrived. That moment when you take a deep nerve-calming breath, get on stage, and effectively communicate to your audience. This chapter will help calm your nerves by totally preparing you for this all-important moment. The lessons learned in this chapter will support you as you confidently make your presentation (Fig. 5.1).

Photo Courtesy of CHISHOLM Inc.

*Figure 5.1   A multimedia presenter uses electronic writing tablet
to write over LCD projected images.*

Yes, you are giving a "multimedia" presentation. But, your desktop computer's screen or overhead projected image is not a substitute for your enthusiasm, energy, and dynamic audience interaction. <u>You</u> are the presenter. Your multimedia presentation will help you communicate more effectively, but it can't establish rapport with your audience, it can't answer questions, and it can't hold their undivided attention for very long. Regardless of whether you make your presentation one-to-one on a computer's screen, or before a small or large group using an overhead projection system, the multimedia presentation is just a tool to help you emphasize your main points and to help your audience retain the message. Keep this in mind as you explore this chapter, so your final product will be polished and professional.

Managing Your Presentation Environment

You take control of your presentation by planning ahead and controlling your presentation environment to the greatest possible extent. This includes considering and handling as many factors as you can <u>before</u> you give the presentation.

Know Thine Audience, and Shift

Consider your audience before you give your presentation. Most multimedia authoring and presentation packages give you the flexibility to tailor your presentation to meet the needs of your audience before and during the presentation. Use this flexibility to delete or add slides and script to mold your presentation directly to your audience. For example, you can use a product-oriented presentation to train salespeople. These salespeople can then slightly modify the presentation to introduce the product to their customers. A slight shift in presentation emphasis makes all the difference.

Facility Considerations

The size of your audience determines the size and type of facility you'll use, and whether or not you'll need assistance to deliver your presentation. Presenting before a large audience requires lots of forethought and planning. If your company doesn't have appropriate facilities, first shop the local hotels to locate a room large enough to accommodate your audience. When looking at a facility, make sure that it offers amenities that make your audience comfortable and at ease. You don't want any loose ends to distract from your presentation.

Take a sketch pad with you when you visit the proposed facility and draw a rough diagram of the room. Indicate the location of the electrical outlets and the lighting and air-conditioning controls so you can plan your equipment and seating arrangement on paper well in advance of the event.

Spend time in the room, get comfortable with its layout, and scope out its "feel" and limitations so you can use this information to your advantage when you make your presentation.

Preparation Checklist

Here's a handy checklist of important facility considerations:

 <u>Electrical Access</u>

- Check the location of all electrical outlets, and plug in a light or another electrical device to make sure they work. Don't wait until the day of your presentation to find out that you don't have electricity! The location of electrical outlets is also critical. Always bring extension cords, and plan for the worst case.

 <u>Lighting</u>

- Ensure that the room has convenient dimmer controls that you or an assistant can use to set the tone of the presentation.

- After the audience is seated, you can dim the house lights while leaving the lighting over you a bit higher, or you can dim all the lights so that the focus is on your visual presentation. <u>Look for a flexible and easy-to-use lighting system.</u>

 <u>Air Conditioning</u>

- Your audience's comfort, without distractions, is key to a successful presentation. Have the room manager turn on the air conditioner, then listen. If it's noisy, you may not be able to use the room. Also make sure that the thermostat works and maintains a constant temperature.

Comfort Zone Assistant

- During the presentation (especially if it's a long one), train an assistant to be responsible specifically for lighting and temperature. This behind-the-scenes helper should be "invisible," so the audience won't be distracted in any way during the presentation.

- Your assistant's mission is to make sure that the room isn't too hot or too cold, that noise is kept to a minimum, that lighting adds to the quality of your presentation, and that everyone is comfortable and attentive. Your mission is to get your point across with no distractions.

Seating Arrangements

- Know how many people are going to attend, and have more than enough chairs set up in advance. Chairs can be fairly close together, almost touching. Ask the hotel's room manger to take care of setup — this should be part of the package when you rent the room. Always have extra chairs stacked at the back of the room to quickly accommodate stragglers and extra people that may show up unexpectedly.

- You or an assistant should greet each person as he or she comes in the door. Ask them to fill up the first rows first. People tend to want to sit in the back rows — you want to make sure that the audience is evenly distributed.

Equipment Setup and Test — Avoid Murphy's Law

Set up and test your equipment on-site before delivering your presentation. Always be prepared with a spare component (overhead projection lamps and fuses), cables, adapters, and a basic tool kit. Do everything you can to avoid Murphy's Law.

Presentation Equipment

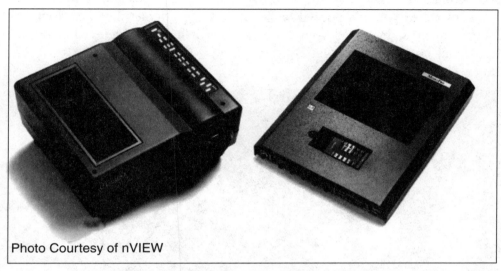

Photo Courtesy of nVIEW

Figure 5.2   LCD Projector and LCD projection panel.

The type of presentation equipment you'll choose depends on the size of your audience, the effects you want to make, and your budget. For standard computerized presentations you'll need:

- A portable or desktop computer with sound capabilities and VGA output. (If you're giving a one-on-one presentation at a client's desk, all you probably need is your presentation on software.)

- An overhead projector with LCD projection panel (active-matrix color is preferred) or an LCD stand-alone projector and screen (Fig. 5.2).

- An electronic writing tablet that allows you to write in color on your projected image is a real plus! (See Fig. 5.1.)

Kodak's Photo CD

If you've created your presentation on Kodak Photo CD using Kodak's *Create-It* or *Arrange-It* authoring packages (or used third-party authoring software) you can put a Kodak Photo CD portable player in your briefcase, bring it with you to your account, plug it into their television set, and give your presentation (Fig. 5.3).

Photo s Courtesy of EASTMAN KODAK

Figure 5.3   *From briefcase to presentation Kodak's portable CD.*

A bevy of presentation equipment is currently available, including LCD projection panels, LCD projectors, electronic writing tablets for highlighting and annotating projected images.

In addition, Chap. 10 presents comprehensive information about Kodak's interactive Photo CD presentation software and equipment.

Use a Flipchart and White-Board Too

Although your primary presentation equipment is computer-related, remember that <u>you</u> are the "primary presentation equipment." To keep your audience awake and interested during the presentation, also use a flipchart and a white-board.

- Use a flip-chart to write down bulleted points for emphasis during the flow of the presentation.
- Use a white-board to list information that you want to remain in front of the audience during the entire presentation.

This "mixed-media" delivery will keep the interest level high and help embed your message in your audience's mind.

Renting Equipment

If you don't want to travel with your own projection and sound equipment, you can ask your hotel to recommend local companies that provide presentation equipment rental and setup services. These people have lots of experience setting up equipment in the room you're going to use. And they are responsible for ensuring that all the equipment works properly so you have a glitch-free presentation.

But, it's still <u>your</u> presentation. Direct the equipment professionals so they know what arrangement you need for your presentation. Don't let them "sell" you on a generic setup just because it may be easier or more familiar to them.

If you decide to bring and set up your own equipment, do a dry run as far in advance of the event as possible. Set up your computer(s), projectors, and screens and walk through the presentation to make sure that all the equipment works the way you want.

Preparation

Know your material so thoroughly, and be so well prepared that you can do your basic presentation without even thinking about it. This requires repeated rehearsal the first time out, but becomes easier and easier each time you make your presentation. You'll even find that subsequent, but different, presentations are easier after you break the ice.

Block out your movements, and give your equipment a thorough workout so you become familiar and comfortable with the physical side of the presentation.

Videotaping your rehearsal is one of the best ways to improve your presentation skills. Be honest with yourself, but don't become your own worst critic. View and evaluate the tape with someone who is more objective and who can give you <u>constructive</u> feedback. Then, work <u>only</u> on those areas that need improvement.

I rehearse with my wife and ten-year-old son, who at times acts as my assistant during presentations. Get someone with whom you feel comfortable and who can give you honest feedback — <u>listen</u>. Always respond to constructive criticism. As a writer, I value a good editor who directs my work and makes suggestions for improvement. My goal is to communicate effectively and concisely — that's your goal too. Evaluate the criticism and incorporate the changes that will make your piece more effective.

Handouts

Handouts can be a valuable addition to your presentation. They can give your audience a convenient way to follow along, a place to write notes, and something to walk away with that reinforces the presentation's message. They are easy to produce (most authorware packages give you lots of flexibility) and give the attendees a tangible item that makes the experience more valuable and memorable.

Knowing when to distribute handouts is important. If you don't want people taking notes during your presentation, don't encourage it by giving out handouts at the outset. Wait until the end. The type of presentation you are making will determine when and what kind of handouts to distribute (Table 5.1).

TABLE 5.1 When to Use Handouts

Handout purpose	Distribution timing
Agenda and backgrounder	Before presentation
Working notes	During presentation
Presentation overview	After presentation

Notes, Scripts, and Index Cards

It's important to maintain rapport and contact with your audience during your presentation without losing your place or your concentration.

After you've reviewed a script, use the projected bulleted points on each slide as your guide to effective presentation. Take a look at Chap. 3's sample scripted presentation. You'll see that each slide's script is summarized in its bullets. Don't ever try to memorize and act out a script word for word. Just use it as a basis to build on, while interjecting your personality, inflection, and pacing.

Be yourself. Speak conversationally, as if you are telling a story to one person. Use the projected bulleted points and 4-by-5 index cards as your guide. Here are a few tips to help you prepare effective index cards:

- One key phrase or point per card — keep each one as simple and as concise as possible.

- Use a heavy black-felt pen and write in heavy letters that can be seen from a distance; leave plenty of white space.

- Number your cards.

- Use your cards to keep you on track and focused.

Be Prepared to Shift

Flexibility is one key to a successful presentation. Be prepared to shift your presentation's flow and direction in response to your audience's needs.

Knowing your audience, listening to them, and knowing what they want will guide you.

Your Mission Statement

Before stepping in front of your audience, declare to yourself (or out loud to your team) the results you intend to achieve at the presentation.

- Set goals and objectives.

- Declare your desired outcome: the results you want to achieve, your "mission statement."

- Declare how you and/or your team are going to "show up" to achieve your presentation's objectives.

- Make your intentions clear to yourself and to your team.

This is your mission statement, and it sets the tone of your presentation and determines how successful the presentation will be. To help make your intentions clear to yourself and to your team, ask these three important questions and write down your responses:

1. What atmosphere do I want to create during this presentation?
2. If there's just one thing that I want the audience to walk away with, what is it?
3. How do I have to show up (be) to make these goals happen (focused, prepared, enthusiastic...)?

The answers to these questions are the bedrock of your presentation. Hold them in your mind -- act on them during the presentation and you <u>will</u> be successful. <u>If you know where you're going, and know how you are going to get there, you'll vastly improve the quality and effectiveness of your presentations.</u>

I recently prepared a presentation for a large company's sales meeting. It was attended by hundreds of sales professionals from around the world. The presentation was one hour, divided between three presenters. To effectively manage their time, I had one person controlling the electronic slides, and asked that each presenter time his presentation to follow each slide's bullet builds. The controller activated each bulleted line of text ahead of the presenter's next point.

Before we began, I reviewed the procedure with each presenter and then asked them to state what they wanted the audience to leave with, what they were going to create, and how they would "show up" to make that happen.

John, an extremely outgoing product market manager, responded jokingly by saying that he "was going to create chaos out there." As it turned out, he wasn't joking.

John grabbed a cordless microphone and walked up and down the aisle like a game-show host with his back to the screen, telling anecdotes, jokes, and stories. He completely departed from the script, totally confused everyone, and created chaos - just like he said he would!

The moral of this story is to make your intentions crystal clear. If your intent is to create chaos, so be it. If your intent is to create a feeling of happiness in the room and have everyone feeling good about your product and your company, you can make that happen, too.

Just be careful what you declare! Your declaration will most likely come true during the presentation - for better or worse.

The Power of Negative Thinking

Don't allow negative thoughts to work their way into your mind before or during the presentation. They're like time bombs, waiting to sabotage your effort. At another presentation, the person I assigned to run the equipment told me that "I know things are going to get messed up. I just know it." Talk about self-fulfilling prophesy! Things did go wrong. Somehow, he pushed the wrong computer keys and got the slide sequence out of order. There are no accidents. He set himself up for this failure by allowing negativism and lack of confidence to creep in.

Everyone, including world-famous operatic tenor Luciano Pavoratti, is nervous before a performance. The trick is to turn this nervous energy into a positive force that makes your presentation explosive and effective. The choice is yours. You can either let your nervousness destroy your presentation or, like the professionals, harness this nervous energy to give you a peak performance edge.

Visualization

Visualization is another powerful preparation technique employed by successful athletes and performers. Before you go on, "watch" yourself delivering a confident presentation.

Mingle—Get to Know Your Audience

Another way to shake those prepresentation nerves is to mingle with your audience before you begin. I always do this. During the presentation I key many of my points and attention to those people whom I spoke to before the presentation began. Doing this helps me to focus and channel my energy, and it will work for you. Just go for it!

Right Before You Go On

Prepare yourself physically by taking a few deep breaths, shaking out tight neck, shoulder and jaw muscles, and walking around to loosen up. Get your throat ready by drinking warm liquids (try to stay away from coffee) and possibly sucking on a lozenge or hard candy. Turn to your audience, smile, and begin when you feel 100% mentally and physically ready, not a moment before.

Presentation Techniques That Work

Lights, Camera, Action!

Lights, camera, action! You know your audience's needs, you've prepared and rehearsed your presentation, all your equipment is working, and the audience is comfortably ready to absorb your message. Calm down! The first thing you must know is that the audience wants you to be successful. They obviously feel that your message will benefit them, or they wouldn't be sitting in their chairs. They want to accept you as the expert and will always give you the benefit of the doubt unless you somehow prove otherwise.

Establishing Ground Rules

Let your audience know what to expect from the presentation, what its structure is, and what the presentation's ground rules are. If you don't want to handle questions until the end of your presentation, tell them. If you are going to have a short break every 30 minutes, tell them. Give them an overview of the presentation's structure, up front, so they know what to expect and what to be prepared for.

Pacing and Basic Timeline Considerations

If you are giving a traditional slide-type presentation, plan to spend about 30 seconds to 1 minute per slide. Make sure to leave time at the end for audience questions and interaction. Use the presentation pacing and timeline chart in Fig. 5.4 as a guide.

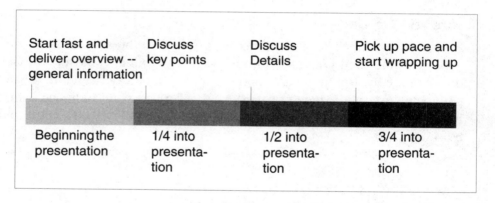

Figure 5.4   Pacing and timing.

Rapport

It takes two to have a successful presentation: you and your audience. You are partners. Observe, listen, and establish rapport. Gauge your audience's mood and feelings during your presentation, and make on-the-fly adjustments to any changes you observe. If they're losing interest, <u>shift</u>; if they look like they don't "get it," <u>shift</u>; if they're enthusiastic and receptive, continue doing what you're doing. It's like a dance. Stay in touch with your partner during your presentation and shift emphasis as you lead them from point to point.

Stand back from the screen to explain each projected visual, so the audience watches you and the screen together. Don't allow the power of multimedia to mesmerize your audience. You'll lose your partner, and your message.

Actions Speak Louder than Words

Believe in yourself, believe in your message, and the audience will believe in you. It is often said that children learn behavioral patterns by observing what their parents <u>do</u> — not what they <u>say</u>.

If you believe what you have to say is important, and you deliver your message with energy, confidence, and conviction, your audience will pick up on your energy and get your message.

Never underestimate the power of nonverbal communications. As much as 70% of your message is conveyed through your body language, the way you hold yourself, and the gestures you make. Stay in touch with your audience with eye contact and nonverbal communication throughout your presentation. It takes two to have a successful presentation: you and the audience. You are partners, and you must gauge moods and feelings during your presentation and adjust on the fly to any observed changes. <u>Remember</u>, if they're losing interest, <u>shift</u>; if they look like they don't "get it," <u>shift</u>; if they're enthusiastic and receptive, continue doing what you're doing. The axiom, "actions speak louder than words," is especially true during your presentation.

Keep your actions and verbal message alive and interesting to engage your audience's attention during your presentation.

Be yourself during the presentation. Don't rigidly choreograph your performance, but do be conscious of your body language. If you loosen your tie or take off your jacket, sit down on the edge of a table, move toward your audience, or lean casually against a stage prop, you convey a sense of intimacy. Conversely, if you walk behind an object and distance yourself from your audience, you convey aloofness and authority - it's your choice. That's why being yourself is always best. You'll never have to worry about delivering conflicting nonverbal messages. However, consciously add just a few appropriate gestures to punctuate important key points and ideas.

Laser-Focus

Avoid telling stories unless you have carefully chosen them for impact and message. You want to deliver information in the most efficient way possible. Laser-focus on your message, and don't dilute it with extraneous stories; unless they are short, make your point better by any other way possible, and help your audience remember your message. Carefully selected stories can be an effective tool; unnecessary storytelling is boring and confusing.

Brightening Up Your Delivery

Be alive and vibrant. Monotone is out! Vary your tone, pitch, volume, and the speed of your delivery to emphasize key elements and to keep your audience involved.

I used to think that I had to raise my voice to make an important point; <u>wrong</u>. I found that speaking softly and slowly was a much better way to emphasize and drive home points. Try contrast. If you naturally tend to speak softly, you can raise your pitch a bit to make your point; if you speak quickly, you can slow down. The way to brighten up your delivery is to consciously shift your inflection to the opposite of the expected mode to make important points.

Pause between phrases and sentences. A run-on delivery conveys to the audience that you just want to get the presentation over with. Pausing and taking your time conveys control.

Handling Disruptions

Handle disruptions or offensive individuals in a businesslike manner. You can tell them that they have a good point, but that you'd like to take it "off-line" so that you can stay on track for all the other people in the audience. Never become defensive, resort to sarcasm, or lose your temper. When you lose your cool, you also lose control of the seminar. Always be businesslike and come back to the overall message you are delivering, and its critical importance to all present.

Fielding Audience Questions

Photo Courtesy of CHISHOLM Inc.

Figure 5.5   Fielding audience questions.

Anticipate and Prepare

During the preparation phase, try to anticipate the most common questions (Fig. 5.5). When you are asked a question, keep your answer short, concise, and to the point. While you are answering, share eye contact between the questioner and the audience so that everyone benefits.

Here are some guidelines to help you make questions reinforce your presentation:

- Focus and listen intently to the questioner.

- Repeat the question without paraphrasing, so the whole audience hears it and you get it.

- If you don't understand the question, or if you think it may be to obtuse for the audience to understand, ask the questioner to restate and clarify the question.

- When you answer the question:

    - Give your answer.

    - Support your answer with background information.

    - Restate and summarize your answer.

- Never bluff! If you don't know the answer to a question, say so. Tell them you'll find the answer and get back to them, or refer them to an expert.

- Ask the audience to solve and suggest answers. Keep your audience involved and participating in the question-and-answer process.

- Ask the questioner if he or she needs any further information or clarification before moving on.

Fielding Hostile Questions

Rarely, but inevitably, someone will ask questions in a challenging and hostile manner. The questioner may be technically correct, but his or her delivery may be openly hostile. Before responding, keep in mind that the hostile individual is not hostile because of you or something you did. He or she is most likely dealing with a personal issue that has nothing at all to do with you or your presentation. Don't take it personally!

Answer calmly and patiently, and attempt to establish a rapport with the individual by asking for clarification, explanation, and elaboration. Agree with the questioner's right to his or her point of view, and shift focus to the facts and away from personalities. Whether or not the person has a legitimate point, thank the individual for his or her input and contribution to the success of the presentation.

Learn from Your Audience

Use question-and-answer sessions to broaden your knowledge of the subject and fine-tune your presentation. It's always a good idea to either record your presentation or have an associate write down the questions and answers so you can include this material in future presentations.

Each presentation you give is a learning experience that you can use to give even better presentations.

The Close

Make a noticeable transition in pace to let your audience know that you are moving into the presentation's close. Review and summarize the ground you've covered to highlight and reinforce the main points you want the audience to walk away with. Issue a call for action, if appropriate, and thank your audience for attending.

You might want to mirror your introduction to close the presentation with finality. I used to begin my presentations by playing a portion of a classical musical piece. I then repeated the same musical piece's finale at the presentation's end while turning up all the lights. You can also effectively end your presentation with quotations or anecdotes that mirror the one that you used at the beginning. Be creative, and think <u>show biz!</u>

Presentation Techniques in Review

Review Checklist

Here is a short checklist of some of the points covered in this chapter. Review it before your presentation to make sure that you've covered the most important issues.

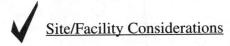

Site/Facility Considerations

- Carefully select your presentation site based on audience size and needs.
- Take care of potential distractions in advance.

Prepare Yourself and Your Team

- Set goals and objectives.

- Declare the desired outcome (results you want to achieve: the "mission statement").

- Declare how you and/or your team are going to achieve your presentation objectives.

- Make your intentions clear to yourself and to your team.

- Rehearse. Become so familiar with your presentation that it becomes part of you.

 ### Presentation Techniques and Considerations

- Laser-focus: Get to your point without unnecessary storytelling.

- Gauge your audience and respond accordingly. Are they with you, or are you losing them?

- Pace your presentation to keep it lively and interesting. Timing is everything!

- Use a mix of computer-generated projected material, a white-board, and a flipchart to keep your audience informed and interested in what you have to say.

 ### Equipment Setup and Test

- Set up and test your equipment on-site before delivering your presentation.

- Be prepared! A spare component, cable adapter, or

screwdriver can save the day.

- Avoid Murphy's Law: Thoroughly prepare in advance.

Microsoft Windows and Multimedia

Microsoft Windows 95, called "Chicago" during development, is designed with multimedia in mind. It moves beyond Windows 3.1 by offering more multimedia features, while <u>maintaining compatibility with all the Windows 3.1 multimedia tools discussed in this book.</u> All the Windows authoring and presentation packages discussed in this book are being updated to take advantage of Windows 95 advanced multimedia features (Fig. 6.1). This translates into faster, better, more powerful authoring and presentation tools for you.[1]

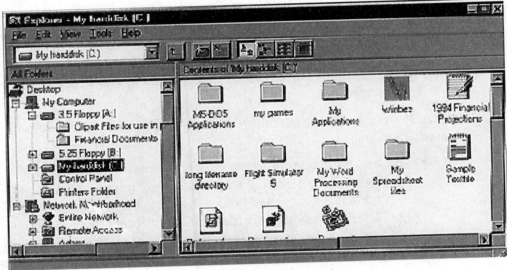

Figure 6.1   *User-friendly interface.*

---

[1] Much of the information in the chapter comes from Microsoft, who were generous enough to allow us to pass it on to you. Windows 95 (Chicago) was in final prerelease testing when this chapter was written, and some of its features may have changed in the final product offering.

Features Overview

Windows 95 makes multimedia presentations easier, more animated, and more engaging.

- <u>Easier</u>. Plug and play (we'll talk more about plug and play later in this chapter) makes it easier to install multimedia devices. All the architectural support for digital video, audio, and MIDI is built into Windows 95, so that users don't have to think about performing setup chores. <u>And Windows 95 is compatible with multimedia titles and tools created for Windows 3.1.</u>

- <u>More animated</u>. Windows 95 is a much better platform for animation-intense computerized presentations than any version of Windows has ever been.

- <u>More engaging</u>. Installing Windows 95 is an immediate multimedia upgrade that allows any PC to become a better, more exciting multimedia playback machine. You can create presentations that are faster and offer more audiovisual excitement.

Windows 95 offers you a powerful authoring platform that yields professional presentation results.

- 32-bit architecture squeezes vastly improved multimedia performance out of PCs, so you can capture digital video and sound that is bigger and bolder than ever before. Windows 95's multitasking architecture (the ability to process more than one job at a time) makes it a much more convenient multimedia-development working environment.

- Custom-designed digital video, digital audio, MIDI, and file-handling subsystems let you create very high quality sound, video, and animation effects. Windows 95 is a very attractive platform for professional development of multimedia effects and footage — even beyond the realm of the PC TV commercials.

Windows 95 Multimedia Features

Plug-and-Play Support

Windows 95 Plug-and-Play makes it easy to install multimedia hardware (like CD-ROMs and sound cards) on your PC. Just plug in a Plug-and-Play-enabled sound card and (literally) it plays without having to set DIP switches, fathom the world of IRQs and interrupts, or reconfigure software. Windows 95 makes installing old multimedia devices much easier, too, by including tools that make it vastly easier to identify and resolve conflicts between devices that are and that are not plug-and-play enabled. Windows 95 also includes built-in drivers for most popular sound cards, which makes adding sound to your system as painless as possible.

Plug and play can put fully equipped multimedia PCs onto virtually every desktop, allowing you to produce presentations with sound, animation, and movies that will be viewed by a wide audience. Plug and play does three things that will help increase your viewing audience:

- It allows the base of multimedia-capable PCs to grow through plug-and-play upgrade kits, rather than placing so much of the growth burden on purchasing new CPUs. Because Windows 95 includes the basic architecture for handling sound, MIDI, and digital video, every Windows 95 PC can easily be made into a multimedia PC by just plugging in a sound card and/or CD-ROM drive. This means that more and more people will have machines that can play your most sophisticated presentations.

- It substantially diminishes the cost of installing and supporting multimedia devices, which will help speed their adoption for business use.

- As multimedia standards (such as CD-ROM speed) continue to improve, plug and play will allow your audience to upgrade multimedia components conveniently without replacing an entire PC. Plug-and-play support will be vital for adoption of new multimedia devices such as MPEG (movie) cards.

AutoPlay — Ship Your Presentations on CD

When you ship a CD-ROM presentation you want it to be as easy as possible to play. With Windows 95, the very act of inserting the disk into the CD-ROM drive begins the presentation.

When you put a disk into a CD-ROM drive, Windows 95 automatically spins it and looks for a file that you've included called AUTORUN.INF; then Windows 95 reads the contents of this file and follows its instructions.

This feature makes setup for a Windows 95–based multimedia presentation virtually automatic — as it should be:

"To play <u>This Presentation,</u> insert the disk into your CD-ROM drive.

Have a nice day!"

Built-in Digital Video Support

Until the release of Windows 95, Microsoft distributed its Video for Windows software package as a stand-alone product. This digital video support package is an integral part of Windows 95 to bring you enhanced multimedia flexibility:

- Because of Windows 95's wide acceptance and use, you can use the .AVI file format to distribute digital video files with the same confidence that you distribute other Windows-supported formats, such as .TXT, .WRI, .BMP, .PCX, and .WAV.

- The barriers to entry for would-be multimedia title and tool developers are lowered because the issues of licensing and installing Microsoft Video for Windows have disappeared. This means that you'll be assured of more and better software tools.

Built-in Sound and MIDI Support

The majority of today's sound cards and built-in sound DSPs have on-board MIDI support and accommodate .WAV sounds — Windows 95 includes built-in support for both MIDI and digitized waveform audio (.WAV).

MIDI is the computer equivalent of a player piano's perforated paper roll. Each hole in the paper instructs the player piano to play a certain note. Similarly, a MIDI file contains textual instructions that control a MIDI synthesizer chip. The chip converts these instructions into synthesized music. The great advantage of MIDI is that the textual instructions occupy very little hard disk space. The instructions for a complete, orchestrated sonata, for example, can reside in a text file that uses only a few kilobytes of storage space. This contrasts to a digitized sound file that can occupy hundreds or thousands of kilobytes. At the high end, MIDI is used as a development tool for musicians. Virtually all advanced music equipment today takes advantage of MIDI's convenient and precise control.

MIDI is becoming ever more popular for multimedia product and presentation development because it allows you to add music with a tiny investment of disk space and data rate. One popular MIDI application (as discussed in Chap. 8) is as lengthy background music to a kiosk presentation.

Windows 95 supports the industry standard general MIDI specification, and comes with Microsoft's best-ever implementation of MIDI, including a new technology called *polymessage MIDI support*. This enhancement allows Microsoft Windows to communicate multiple MIDI instructions simultaneously within a single interrupt. Polymessage MIDI support requires less computing power than it did before, and allows developers to successfully process MIDI instructions concurrently with graphics and other data.

Built-in Virtual CD Player

The controls on the Windows 95 virtual CD player look just like a home CD player, and it supports many of the same features you find in advanced CD players (such as random play, programmable playback order, and the ability to save programs) so that you don't have to recreate your playlist each time you pop in a CD. You can ship CD presentations and music to anyone using Windows 95 and know that they'll be able to take advantage of it.

Fast DIB Drawing Means Smoother Presentations

A 32-bit call added to the Windows 95 Win32 API CreateDIBSection allows developers to get bit maps onto the screen as quickly as possible if there is nothing fancy (such as clipping or stretching); the CreateDIBSection call actually allows applications to send DIBs more or less directly to the video frame buffer.

To accommodate quality presentations, a portion of Windows 95 CreateDIB-Section improvements have also been moved into a tool for Windows 3.1, called the *WinG libraries*. WinG libraries allow developers to create fast graphical games and presentation software in a Windows 3.1 environment with full compatibility into Windows 95.

Engaging Multimedia with 32-Bit Digital Video Playback

Displaying digital video involves moving and processing huge streams of data continuously and efficiently. Windows 95 digital video implementation offers exciting efficiencies that allow software developers to confidently create multimedia titles that are smoother and cleaner than ever before.

Multimedia title originators, presentation creators, and game developers are businesspeople who create a product to reach the most people with the best product. Until the introduction of Windows 95, developers were forced to include lowest-common-denominator digital video to ensure that as many PCs as possible could play their presentation, title, or game. Developers have tended to use postage-stamp-sized video windows with low frame rates (which make movement look jerky) and extreme compression (which makes the video look blocky).

Windows 95 raises the lowest common denominator significantly. In the past, the process of displaying digital video relied on a series of 16-bit systems for reading data from disk, decompressing the video data, and displaying it on screen. One key design goal of Windows 95 was to transition this architecture to 32 bits, and the difference is eye-popping. For multimedia users, installing Windows 95 will be the quickest and cheapest multimedia upgrade available. Without adding any hardware, Windows 95 enables customers to display bigger, smoother, more colorful digital video than ever before (Fig. 6.2).

Figure 6.2   Multiple applications.

It's also important to note that Windows 95 multimedia is fully compatible with 16-bit multimedia titles. Testing has shown that the 32-bit improvements in file access speed and stream handling results in performance improvements even for 16-bit multimedia applications. The biggest improvements, of course, will be realized in the new generation of fully 32-bit presentation creation software and titles designed for Windows 95. You can expect that most Windows-compatible multimedia authoring packages will be upgraded to let you take advantage of this power.

Windows 95 also contains an improved display driver to enhance performance.

Multitasking and Threads: No Interruptions Please...

Multimedia applications don't take well to interruption. When you are watching a video clip or listening to a sound file, you really don't want it to stop in the middle.

The multitasking in Windows 95 is quite different from prior versions of Windows because it is preemptive. In Windows 95, multiple 32-bit processes can share the CPU at the same time, whether those processes have been initiated by different applications (multitasking) or by one application (threading).

This has a very important implication for how your multimedia presentation will feel to your audience. Threading gives your presentations a smoother, finished feeling. For example, a kiosk presentation might have a thread that plays background music continuously — 32-bit processing helps smooth out the breaks between scenes and when the presentation is loading new data on another thread of the program.

As applications, tools, and codecs (file compression standards) are rewritten to 32 bits, video and other multimedia processes will become less and less likely to be interrupted by other applications. An example of this is that in Windows 95 you can move a video window while it is playing with no interruptions!

Built-in Support for Fast CD-ROMs

The trend toward faster CD-ROM drives (double- and triple-speed) is a very good thing for multimedia computing. To get the best possible performance from these new devices, Windows 95 includes a new 32-bit CD-ROM file system (CDFS) for reading files from CD-ROM drives as quickly and efficiently as possible. The Windows 3.1 system for reading files from CD-ROM drives (MSCDEX.DLL) is included in Windows 95 to ensure compatibility with products that rely on it.

Reading CD-ROM data faster helps make video and audio playback from CD-ROM drives look and sound better. This is an important component of the overall performance enhancements to multimedia in Windows 95.

Windows 95 also extends its support for CD-ROM to drives that read XA-encoded disks, such as Kodak PhotoCD and Video CDs.

MPEG Hardware Support for TV-like Video from Your CD-ROM

The MPEG codec (compression/decompression system) squeezes digital video and stereo audio into an incredibly small data stream. For example, a feature movie compressed using MPEG can fit on two CD-ROMs.

Displaying video from an MPEG file is so calculation-intensive that the only practical way to display MPEG video on today's PCs is by using hardware assistance. Together with the Open PC MPEG Consortium, Microsoft has defined an industry standard for MPEG board and chip makers that want to ship MPEG devices for Windows 95. This translates into more options for you. With this standard in place, you can add MPEG video to your productions knowing that it can be widely distributed and viewed, without worrying about precisely which vendor's MPEG device is present to decompress it.

Sound Compression for CD-Quality Sound

Sound can take up a lot of disk space. Full CD-quality, uncompressed audio contains a lot of data — about 176K for every second of sound! An entire CD-ROM can contain only a little over an hour of music. It can also eat up a fair-sized chunk of the data rate that a CD-ROM drive is capable of sustaining.

To lessen the burden of storing and playing sound from an application, Windows 95 includes a family of sound-compression technologies (codecs). These codecs can be divided into two groups:

- Music-oriented codecs (such as IMADPCM) are included that allow close to CD-quality sound to be compressed to about one-quarter size.

- Voice-oriented codecs (such as TrueSpeech) are included to allow very, very efficient compression of voice data.

This support for compressed sound is two-way. You can play sound from a compressed sound file or you can compress a sound file (using the built-in sound-recording and editing utility). If you have a microphone, you can turn on voice compression when recording so that your file is compressed in real time.

In addition to the codecs that come with Windows 95, the audio architecture of Windows multimedia is designed to be extendible through other installable codecs. The video architecture of Windows multimedia can be extended in the same way.

Capturing and Compressing Digital Video

Video contains an enormous amount of data. Capturing digital video is even more data-intensive than playing it back, because raw digital video footage is uncompressed. A single frame of full-color video at 640 6 480 contains close to a megabyte of data. At 30 frames per second, you can fill up a 1-gigabyte hard drive with uncompressed video data in less than a minute. There are ways to compress this data to make your storage go further, but the rate at which you can write data to disk is of even greater importance.

Windows 95's 32-bit file access is as important to digital video authors as it is to digital video users. Because you can write more data to disk more quickly in Windows 95, you can capture better-looking video that is bigger, has more frames per second, and is more colorful.

Once the raw footage is captured, the compression step is a potentially time-consuming process. Both Cinepak and Indeo compression are available in 32-bit versions for Windows 95 to make the process considerably more efficient.

Built-in Support for Multimedia Devices

Windows 95 includes built-in support for common multimedia authoring devices such as laser disks and VCRs. This makes it easy to set up a system for step capture, a process in which the author captures digital video data one frame at a time, usually to be compressed later. This is a slow process, but it is absolutely the best way to get the best-possible-quality digital video.

Frame-accurate control of a VCR is also important for recording broadcast-quality special effects to use in commercials, movies, television programs, music multimedia PCs, and videos.

The Future of Windows 95 Multimedia Products

Microsoft is working with industry to make your multimedia authoring and presentation environment the best it can be. Here's a list of Microsoft recommendations to OEMs (Original Equipment Manufacturers), so you can glimpse into future multimedia trends:

- Multimedia playback places heavy demands on many parts of the system, from the CD-ROM (reading data) to the hard disk (writing data) to the CPU (decompressing) to the video and audio subsystems (playing it). A fast CPU does not guarantee a great playback system. In fact, multimedia playback on most of today's high-end PCs is not constrained by the CPU.

- Local bus video is indispensable. Even OEMs creating nonmultimedia systems should use local bus video, because doing so will enable consumers to plug-and-play their way to a multimedia system later, should they choose to do so. Without local bus video, a PC will not be able to keep up with the amount of video data that multimedia titles and games will want to display continuously.

- Double-speed CD-ROM or better. Titles will be written assuming double-speed data rates.

- SVGA (800 6 600) or better with 16-bit color. Why more colors than 256? Because multimedia applications use a lot of colors and tend to compete for access to the system palette. Consider the challenge of a multimedia presentation that includes a digital video clip of an underwater scene on a slide with a smooth-shaded maroon background. There aren't enough colors in a 256-color palette to make both the slide background and the underwater scene look good.

- 16-bit audio. The installed base of sound cards that can interpret MIDI is now large enough to be tempting to presentation, game, and title developers. Not all sound systems are equal - some sound great (16-bit with sampled sounds) and some don't. The differences are significant, and customers will be able to tell the difference.

Recommendations to Industry for Great-Sounding Audio

There is a great deal of variation in the quality of audio cards and sound systems. Most of the time, sound cards up to now have been used principally for their ability to play waveform audio the equivalent of recorded sound. For some uses, like voice-overs, there is no realistic alternative to recorded waveforms. However, recorded sound is very resource-intensive for both the CD-ROM and the CPU. In Windows 95, there are enhancements to the handling of MIDI that makes it an even more appealing alternative to .WAV for playing music within games and multimedia titles. There are several things that makers of audio cards and systems can do to distinguish themselves:

- Polymessage MIDI support. This is a very efficient new technology included in Windows 95 that makes it easier for application and game writers to use MIDI. If a sound card supports polymessage MIDI, the CPU use required to play even a very complex song is quite small.

- 16-voice or better polyphony. Polyphony is the ability to play multiple sounds at once. Support for more concurrent sounds means fuller-sounding playback.

- Sampled sound rather than waveform synthesis. Waveform synthesis uses a mathematical approximation of a sound, such as a piano. Sampled sound is an actual recording of the piano, and sounds considerably better. Including samples of at least the most common General MIDI instruments helps ensure that music in games and titles sounds really good, instead of synthetic.

Recommendations to Industry for Enhanced Video

Recently, Microsoft released a new DCI display driver. This technology was developed in partnership with Intel and other makers of advanced video display cards.

DCI is a device-driver-level interface that allows Windows to take advantage of hardware features that are (or could be) built into advanced display adapters, specifically:

- Stretching, which speeds up rendering of images that are stretched or distorted

- Color-space conversion, which assists in playback of compressed digital video by accepting YUV data instead of requiring RGB

- Double buffering, which allows faster, smoother block transfers (BLTs) of images by providing memory space for off-screen drawing

- Chroma key, which facilitates the merging of video data streams, allowing a particular color to be treated as transparent in the merge operation

- Overlay, which speeds display of partly concealed objects

- Asynchronous drawing, which, along with double buffering, provides a faster method for drawing into off-screen memory space

Most of the hardware features above relate to the fast, efficient decompression and playback of digital video. Applications that use the Microsoft Video for Windows architecture will benefit from these features automatically and substantially.

Recommendations to Industry for Better Graphics

There are four kinds of graphics an application might want to draw on the screen, and four APIs that an application can use to do so:

- Productivity application graphics. Scroll bars, fonts, buttons, and the like. Applications that want the system to help them draw these things use GDI, the basics Windows graphics API.

- Digital video. Applications that want to play digital video use the Video for Windows API. More details on the Video for Windows architecture are provided in the following section.

- Game graphics. Games draw their own graphics (in memory) and want bit maps blasted to the screen as fast as possible. That's what WinG does. It is available for Windows 3.1, and provides many of the same benefits of Windows 95's CreateDIBSection function, as well as fast access to the frame buffer through DCI.

- 3D engineering graphics. Applications that want the system to help them draw 3D solids use OpenGL. OpenGL is Microsoft's strategic choice of 3D application programming interface. We have a long-term commitment to deliver an implementation of OpenGL as part of the broader Win32 API.

There are three pieces to the device driver interface in Windows, and the APIs described above are designed to take advantage of whichever DDI provides the best performance.

- GDI-DDI is the basic graphics device driver interface for Windows. It is optimized for the flexible graphics requirements described above for the GDI API.

- DCI is the new device driver interface created jointly by Microsoft and Intel. DCI drivers provide a fast, direct way for games and digital video in windows to write to the video frame buffer. It also enables digital video playback to take advantage of several specific kinds of hardware support included on advanced graphics adapters. For example, stretching hardware can allow users to scale up the size of a digital video clip with virtually no additional strain on the CPU. Color space conversion support in hardware can reduce the amount of work a codec must perform by up to 30%, allowing substantially better video playback.

- The 3D-DDI will enable applications that use OpenGL to take advantage of accelerated 3D support in hardware.

Summing Up

Windows 95 has moved the multimedia state of the art one giant step forward with enhancements in graphics, animation, digital video, and sound (Fig. 6.3). With Windows 95 your presentations play smoother, have a more professional look and sound, and will be received by a wider audience. Your software authoring tools and presentation software is also evolving to take advantage of 32-bit processing to make your job easier and the results more effective.

Figure 6.3   Putting multimedia to work on Windows 95.

Introduction

Apple Computer's[1] continued innovation in both hardware and software is a major driving force behind the rapid growth and acceptance of multimedia.

Multimedia is the integration of text, graphics, sound, animation, and video. The interactive multimedia solutions discussed in this book provide new, more effective access to information and communication. As you can see in Chaps. 8 and 9, companies are rapidly making a transition from analog information to the world of digital information to take advantage of these new technologies.

This chapter provides an in-depth look at Apple Computer's tools, products, concepts, and the vision they have for bringing this world of digital information to the widest possible audience (Fig. 7.1). You'll see where Apple was yesterday, where it is today, and discover where it is headed tomorrow so you can plan your multimedia future.

Figure 7.1   Apple Macintosh audiovisual computer.

Why Apple for Multimedia?

Apple Computer holds a number of significant advantages for developers

---

[1] Apple Computer was generous enough to provide much of the information presented in this chapter. All photos in this chapter are courtesy of Apple Computer.

of interactive, media-rich applications and titles, as well as for consumers of multimedia products. From the sound integration in the very first Macintosh computers to the introduction of digital video, built-in CD-ROM drives, speech technologies, and communications capabilities, the Macintosh has been, in a very real sense, the first "multimedia computer." The Macintosh is designed as the ideal platform for the development and playback of multimedia applications for multiple platforms. Advantages of the Macintosh for multimedia include:

- Ease of use through tight integration of hardware and software. The ability to integrate text, sound, and graphics has always been built into every Macintosh computer, making the Macintosh well suited for advanced applications such as multimedia authoring and presentation. Apple has extended this capability with richer time-based media such as video. Advanced software technology such as the industry-standard QuickTime—is designed to take advantage of Macintosh hardware so that both developers and users can create and deliver media-rich applications.

- Advanced multimedia technology and tools. Many of the industry's leading-edge multimedia technology and tools are designed for the Macintosh platform. For example, some of the best desktop tools for developing graphics, sound, and video are written for Macintosh systems. Similarly, CD-ROM drives attached to Macintosh computers are able to take immediate advantage of the built-in sound and graphic capabilities, whereas the CD-ROM drives attached to most other computer systems can only deliver text-based information unless the CPU is modified with a third-party's video cards, sound cards, and other peripherals.

- Cross-platform development and delivery. Apple provides a unique platform for true cross-platform development of media-rich applications. Apple's strategy is to provide an ideal environment that allows designers and programmers to develop and deliver cost-effective applications to multiple platforms. In contrast, technology on most other platforms dictates that developers create and deliver products on only one system.

Some Background:
The Hakone Forum - Defining a Global Strategy for New Media

In 1992, Apple Computer hosted the Hakone Forum in Japan to share the results of Harvard University's converging industries study with the highest level of industry influencers from around the world, in such diverse fields as computers, telecommunications, consumer electronics, publishing, entertainment, and education, as well as individual visionaries, authors, and other members of the creative community. The purpose of the forum was to shape the future of New Media, to discuss the ways that technology was bringing together markets and forms of expression that had previously been unrelated, and to examine the ways in which the convergence of industries was affecting the future of their term for multimedia, "New Media."

Together, the members of the Hakone Forum identified a few critical areas in which multimedia developers and industries must search for answers as they create these new opportunities:

- Standards. It is obvious that the number of platforms for multimedia development and playback is not decreasing, but is growing rapidly. In addition, the individual platforms are becoming increasingly complex. For example, in the case of CD-ROM development, multimedia developers constantly need to cope with over 25 different standards — from White-Book to Yellow-Book to Red-Book, etc.— with more standards likely on the way. The situation is likely to deteriorate with more and more platforms entering the market, making it that much more difficult for the developer.

- Salability. Developers for the multimedia market currently must second-guess technologies and platforms for which to develop products, since standards have not yet stabilized. The ideal solution for multimedia developers would be to develop once (on one platform) and deliver the product many times (on many platforms) using one underlying set of technologies and scripting or programming language that provides for a scalable format across systems.

- Lessons from the traditional publishing industry. Where can multimedia developers look for guidance in an industry that did not even exist a few years ago? The answer is to look to the traditional publishing industry for lessons in the content as well as the publishing process.

After establishing a successful dialog the participants of the Hakone Forum developed a number of action items to drive future initiatives. These action items included:

- Creating enabling platforms for New Media production

- Building a New Media center

- Creating a mutual forum for continuing exchanges regarding New Media

- The goal of working toward a "hypernetwork society"

- Establishing a media and publishing stakeholders' work group

- Creating a working group on New Media for children, education and learning

- The conclusions from the Hakone Forum are the basis for a significant portion of Apple Computer's strategy for the New Media market, as described in the following section.

Apple's New Media Strategy

Apple's goal is to provide superior technologies, tools, titles, and applications for developing and delivering New Media. Later in this chapter, we describe Apple's current multimedia offerings and point to products that may be developed in the future. The basic structure of Apple's New Media strategy is divided into fixed broad areas: technology, tools, titles, and applications. Within these three areas, New Media products are developed and delivered to vertical market segments such as home, education, and business.

Technology

At the foundation of this New Media strategy are Apple's enabling hardware and software technologies: the Macintosh and Power Macintosh computers, audio/visual-capable Macintosh computers, QuickTime, and QuickTime for Windows. From the outset, Apple computers and other technologies have been designed to facilitate basic multimedia functions that integrate text, graphics, sound, animation and video.

For consumers, Apple offers low-cost CD-ROM-configured systems that — from the moment they are unpacked — are integrated, multimedia-capable machines. Users of Macintosh systems do not have to add soundboards, communications capabilities, or other add-ons. For owners of Macintosh computers without CD-ROMs, Apple offers multimedia upgrade kits, allowing users to easily expand their systems to be CD-ROM-configured. Apple also offers upgrade kits for Windows-based PCs.

For developers, Apple provides both hardware and software technologies-ranging from powerful Macintosh workstations to QuickTime™ and Quick-Time™ for Windows. Apple technologies are designed to allow developers to create not only for Macintosh, but for other platforms, to make sure that developers maximize their return on investment.

Tools

A wide range of third-party and complementary Apple tools are enabled by the baseline Apple technologies. These tools facilitate the development of multimedia products on Macintosh computers for delivery on Macintosh systems as well as other platforms.

As Apple technologies expand to include deliverable capabilities for other platforms for example, QuickTime™ for Windows — the availability of Macintosh tools for development of titles and applications also grows exponentially. Initially, Apple is focusing on developing for Macintosh and Microsoft Windows platforms. In the future, Apple, along with its third parties, may look into expanding this base of technologies and tools to additional platforms such as game machines and interactive television.

Titles and Applications

Apple technology and tools enable developers to create compelling titles and applications. New Media delivery applications such as kiosks, videoconferencing, presentations, reference; titles and desktop video are growing quickly.

New Media Development

To create interactive multimedia titles from consumer education, business presentations, and game titles to in-house referencing and training materials a developer needs a combination of technology and tools specifically designed for interactive media. These requirements include a system with the necessary speed and power, audio/visual capabilities, and great multimedia tools to facilitate development. Because of Apple's leadership in technology for sound, graphics, and video production, Macintosh computers are ideal platforms for developing media-rich content.

Many developers have selected the Macintosh as the multimedia development system of choice for a number of compelling reasons: because of the suite of tools available for the Macintosh, the ability to develop easily using CD-ROM drives with Macintosh systems, and the media-rich development environment of the Macintosh computer itself.

Apple has focused on assisting developers through the following programs:

- Apple Multimedia Program (AMP). The Apple Multimedia program is an effective resource and clearinghouse for multimedia developers. The program meets the needs of multimedia title publishers, production services companies, information/content providers, in-house developers, and multimedia systems integrators and consultants.

  Members receive quarterly mailings with marketing and technical information consisting of market research reports, product information, and multimedia guidebooks such as *Demystifying Multimedia*, a guide to developing multimedia products. There is a "Members Only" folder on the AppleLink electronic mail service that contains information such as monthly discounts on third-party products and guides on multimedia authoring and marketing. There are also quarterly events for members that focus on multimedia-specific issues.

- New Media centers. The New Media centers were launched by the Apple New Media Mission, U.S. Higher Education, and ApplesSoft teams in conjunction with consortium partners Macromedia, SONY, Adobe, FWB, Paramount, and Supermac.

  These centers are located on university/college campuses around the world, and are designed to stimulate the creation of model learning centers for interactive media technologies. The New Media centers are equipped with hardware, software, and peripheral products for multimedia development and production. They serve not only the students and faculty of the participating institutions but are also open to local multimedia developers, artists, business professionals, and other members of the community.

Multimedia CD-ROM Technology and More

Currently, many multimedia products are delivered and stored using CD-ROM disks and drives. Small and portable CD-ROM disks can store large amounts of data, making it possible to deliver text, graphics, sound animation, and video.

CD-ROM technology is only the first step in multimedia delivery and storage.

As technology for storing and distributing media-rich data improves, large media servers will become widely available. These servers will allow multimedia information to be distributed via network-based computer systems. In the future, as the networking infrastructure evolves, media storage is likely to move to a more traditional client/server architecture, much like the data storage servers we see today.

Apple Technology Today

Hardware Technology

At the heart of Apple's multimedia strategy are the Macintosh computers themselves, ranging from PowerBook to Performa systems and high-performance Power Macintosh computers. Since Apple has integrated multimedia design features such as sound, video-ready connections, and networking capabilities into the architecture of its personal computers, all Macintosh computers are multimedia-capable machines.

Audiovisual (AV) Technologies

In 1993, Apple introduced a line of integrated AV systems. These computers integrate telecommunication and video technologies in a powerful desktop computer. Users can display full-motion video, digitize and capture single frames as pictures or video sequences, and take advantage of built-in video, text to speech, on-board audio media capabilities, and GeoPort, which provides a link to telephone services.

PowerMacintosh

With the introduction of Power Macintosh computers, Apple delivers high-speed, smooth presentation performance and flexibility.

For the multimedia developer, native Power Macintosh applications bring a new level of speed and efficiency to development on the desktop, in areas like digital video compression and special effects.

Apple's first Power Macintosh computers are mid-range and high-end Macintosh models. In succeeding generations, PowerPC versions of Apple's product line will be offered, from the Macintosh Quadra, Macintosh (Centris™ to Performa, Classic, IIC, IC, and PowerBooks™).

CD-ROM Drives

CD-ROM technology is the predominant delivery and storage medium of today's multimedia systems. Apple was among the first to recognize the importance of this technology, introducing its first CD-ROM drive in 1988 (Fig. 7.2).

Figure 7.2   AppleCD 300e Plus external CD-ROM.

AppleCD 300e Plus. The AppleCD 300e Plus external CD-ROM player extends the capabilities of the successful 300 series of CD-ROM drives. At 342 Kbps streaming data transfer rate, it is among the fastest double-speed players on the market. A 256-Kb cache memory allows the drive to transfer information at up to 2.5 Mb per second, giving it nearly the performance of today's triple-speed CD-ROM players.

Like all 300-series CD-ROM drives, the AppleCD 300 CD-ROM drive is a high-speed, high-performance drive with the built-in capability to support new CD-ROM formats as well as Kodak's PhotoCD. Using PhotoCD technology, users can view, zoom in, rotate, crop, and store images on a Macintosh. Users can also cut and paste images from a CD-ROM disc into their word processing, presentation, and graphics documents. The AppleCD 300e Plus also lets users play back QuickTime™ movies, video, and animation, listen to standard CD audio disks, and even transfer CD digital audio data over SCSI connections to a Macintosh for future editing.

QuickTake

The Apple QuickTake 100 digital camera for the Macintosh lets users take 24-bit, high-quality color pictures and quickly load them into a Macintosh computer (Fig. 7.3). This affordable digital camera, and its predecessors, need no film. Users can shoot 32 standard-resolution images or 8 high-resolution images at a time, and then--using the included serial cable and software--load the images into a Macintosh computer where they can be displayed on a monitor in more than 16 million colors.

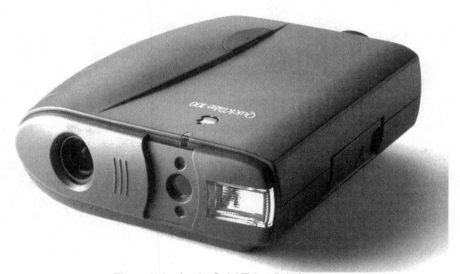

Figure 7.3   Apple QuickTake digital camera.

Weighing about a pound with batteries installed, the QuickTake camera is both convenient and easy to use. Easy-to-read icons on the display panel monitor flash and battery status, the number of pictures taken and remaining, selected resolution, self-timer settings, and more. The possibilities for adding impact to the images are unlimited. Once images are transferred to the Macintosh, you can select and view multiple thumbnail images, delete the ones you don't want, then rotate, crop, scale, and zoom in. Save images in PICT, TIFF, or QuickTake file formats, and then paste the images into word processing, database, presentation, or publishing applications.

AppleDesign Powered Speakers

Figure 7.4   AppleDesign powered speakers.

Sound is critical to the multimedia experience; Apple Computer's AppleDesign Powered Speakers were the first speakers specifically designed for the personal computer providing audiophile-quality sound with an innovative industrial design (Fig. 7.4). The speakers can enhance the user's multimedia experience on the computer, or add excellent stereo sound to the multitude of personal electronic products or televisions in today's home. Magnetic shielding reduces interference, so customers can use them near their monitor and peripheral devices.

Apple Multimedia Kit for Macintosh

The new Apple Multimedia Kit for Macintosh is aimed at users who want to bring a complete multimedia solution to their Macintosh. In addition to Apple's new external CD-ROM player and new AppleDesign Powered Speakers 11, the kit includes Apple Headphones, Compton's Interactive Encyclopedia for Macintosh, all required cables, setup software, and the customer's choice of up to three free CD-ROM titles from a list of more than 30 top-selling discs. The Apple Multimedia Kit upgrades existing Macintosh computers including Performa and Power Macintosh — into complete multimedia systems.

Multimedia Kit for Windows

Figure 7.5   Multimedia Kit for Windows.

The Multimedia Kit for Windows includes the AppleCD 300i Plus (an internal version of the CD-ROM player), AppleDesign Powered Speakers, Apple Headphones, Compton's Interactive Encyclopedia for Windows, a MediaVision 16-bit sound card, all required cables, setup software, and the consumer's choice of up to three free CD-ROM titles (Fig. 7.5).

FireWire: A Faster, Better Serial Bus

Apple's New Media division has released FireWire, a digital data interface design that promises to standardize communication between devices.

FireWire is a peripheral I/O interconnect that provides fast, real-time, active distributed serial bus. Known as SCSI-3 in the disk drive community, FireWire is Apple's implementation of a new industrial standard, the IEEE P1394 High Speed Serial Bus.

FireWire complements the other two environments of electronic plumbing: the backplane and the IAN. What the customer sees is a small, attractive connector that seems to wire everything together into a single system. This advanced serial bus has been licensed to a number of leading-edge manufacturers, including NCR Corporation and Texas Instruments.

Software Technology

Apple's multimedia commitment is exemplified by its development and continuing support for QuickTime software—an enabling multimedia technology that is rapidly becoming <u>the</u> cross-platform multimedia standard.

QuickTime

QuickTime is Apple's software architecture that takes media-rich content beyond the Macintosh to other platforms (Fig. 7.6). QuickTime is an enabling technology that allows integration of media (such as sound, video, and animation) in a consistent, seamless fashion to personal computers and consumer electronic devices. QuickTime is the only architecture that can deliver multimedia content across multiple platforms.

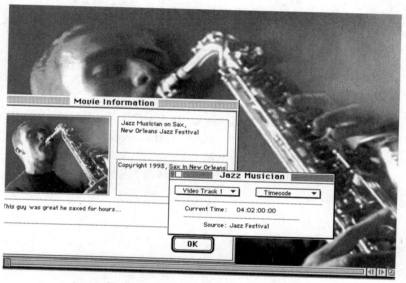

Figure 7.6   QuickTime 2.0 in action.

QuickTime is available for Macintosh, Windows, and FM-Towns machines from Fujitsu.

QuickTime 2.0 makes creating a whole new generation of CD titles and applications a reality. It allows users to view full-size video that closely resembles a television view, at fast frame rates, without the need for video boards. The faster video and data in/out represents a 300% increase over the previous version of QuickTime. QuickTime 2.0 also supports music and interactive television. Music tracks, including a library of MIDI sounds licensed from Roland Corporation, are much smaller than that of standard digital audio formats, allowing disk space to be conserved. Music movies are also midi-compatible.

To support Apple's interactive television efforts, QuickTime 2.0 also supports MPEG1 (Motion Picture Experts Group) video compression scheme for both development and delivery. MPEG is an ISO standard, cooperatively developed by more than 70 companies and institutions worldwide, including Sony, Philips, Matsushita, and Apple. It is expected to become the digital video standard for CDs, cable television, direct satellite broadcast, and high-definition television. The modular architecture of QuickTime will allow it to also support the MPEG2 standard when it becomes available in the near future.

Virtual Reality with QuickTime VR

QuickTime VR is software that enables a user to view a photographic or rendered representation of a scene in 360° view (Figs. 7.7 and 7.8). Users can zoom in or out of a scene, navigate from one scene to another, and even "pick up" objects. Correct perspective is maintained as the user changes his or her view of the scene, giving the effect of being at the center of the action and looking around.

Figure 7.7 QuickTime VR wide angle view.

Apple expects QuickTime VR to be widely adopted by CD-ROM title developers, architectural planners, engineering application developers, and game manufacturers. They also see it making its way into business presentations in the future. Just imagine being able to give clients a panoramic tour of your company—with them at the center of the action!

Figure 7.8   QuickTime VR normal perspective view of same scene.

Multimedia Authoring and Presentation Tools

HyperCard

Back in 1987, Apple began to provide multimedia development capabilities for the Macintosh by introducing HyperCard. HyperCard organizes information into easy-to-use "stacks" of cards through which users can navigate and search for the information they need. Simply by clicking on a button, users view related text, see a graphic, hear a sound, or, in the current version of HyperCard, watch a QuickTime movie. The 2.2 version of HyperCard provides significant enhancements over previous versions, including Applescript support and color. Applescript support allows users to automate repetitive tasks by launching, controlling, and exchanging data with other scriptable applications.

HyperCard is an ideal development tool for a wide range of applications, including multimedia presentations, front ends to host data, courseware, and computer-based training materials. And its compatibility with Apple's World-Script system extension helps developers create multilingual solutions easily.

Using HyperTalk, AppleScript, or any scripting language compatible with Apple's Open Scripting Architecture (OSA), developers can write scripts and attach them to HyperCard buttons to launch, control, and exchange data with other off-the-shelf scriptable applications, either locally or over a network. This lets developers create HyperCard applications that automate repetitive tasks, such as collecting data from multiple sources and generating reports. A new option in version 2.2 lets you save any stack as a stand-alone double-clickable Macintosh application that can be distributed without royalty fees.

Familiar Macintosh interface elements make HyperCard so easy to learn that beginners can start creating stacks right away. HyperCard also offers extensive on-line help, as well as ready-to-use stacks, templates, and elements.

HyperCard provides a robust prototyping and development environment for professional developers. It comes with powerful scripting tools, a modeless script editor, hypertext support, debugging tools, external commands, and many other features to help you create powerful custom software and dynamic presentations.

Apple Media Kit

One of the lessons brought forth at the Hakone Forum on multimedia was the concept that New Media products will be created not only by traditional technology developers, but also by creative designers. Therefore, specialized tools for New Media development are required: easy-to-use creative tools for designers and powerful development tools for programmers.

The Apple Media Kit as overviewed in this book is a complete object-based multimedia authoring solution for cross-platform development. It is composed of two main components: the Media Tool, for creative designers, and the Media Tool Programming Environment, for creative programmers.

The Media Tool allows designers to assemble media elements and add interactivity to projects without scripting. Whether media elements are PICT images, QuickTime movies, sound, or text, designers can exercise their creativity when creating multimedia products without being held back by possible limitations in programming knowledge. If additional interactivity is needed, the project is easily transported to the Media Tool Programming Environment for further enhancement by programming professionals.

The second component, the Media Tool Programming Environment, is a fully object-oriented programming environment that allows programmers to customize and add capabilities to the projects created with the Apple Media Tool.

The Apple Media Tool Programming Language allows developers to generate code that:

- Is portable across both Macintosh and Windows platforms

- Is highly maintainable

- Is easily integrated with other languages such as C

Examples of Media Tool Programming Environment enhancements include creating a database search engine for an electronic catalog on a network; adding speech technology to a program; conditional branching based on user input; adding functionality from the Macintosh toolbox or Windows toolbox; and adding high-performance Sprite animation.

Third-Party Media Creation, Integration, and Production Tools

A wide variety of third-party vendor products are available for the Macintosh, including products from such leading vendors as Macromedia, Adobe Systems, Aldus, Sony, Kodak, and many others introduced to you in this book.

For media capture and creation, designers can use products that digitize photographs, videos, sound, and text.

Apple Media Authoring Solution

The Apple Media Authoring Solution consists of hardware and software tools that enable developers to use animation, 3D modeling, special video effects and object-oriented authoring to create CD-ROM titles, multimedia presentations, video kiosks, and games. This capability is for the multimedia expert producer and is more than you'll probably ever need for producing multimedia business presentations.

The solution provides all the necessary tools to create CD-ROMs compatible with the Macintosh and, with the addition of a simple software tool, developers can use the same system to develop disks for use with Windows, 3DO, and Philips CDI.

The Apple Media Authoring solution is designed for use with Macintosh Quadra computers. The bundled system features include:

- SuperMac's DigitalFilm video card and ThunderStorm s/w acceleration card

- AppleDesign Powered Speakers

- Apple Media Tool

- Adobe Premiere Deluxe CD-ROM Edition and Adobe Photoshop Deluxe CD-ROM edition

- CoSA After Effects

- Macromedia Director, MacroModel, Action!, Sound Edit Pro and DECK II, and other editing and authoring tools

- Macromedia MacroModel — three-dimensional, spline-based modeling software

- ClipMedia

- Kodak Shoebox and Kodak Portfolio CD authoring

The competitively priced Apple Media Authoring Solution is ideal for corporate content developers, training departments, interactive kiosk developers, CD-ROM developers, electronic game designers, public relations and advertising agencies, graphic designers, animators, and 3D modelers.

Apple Professional Video Production Solution

The Apple Professional Video Production Solution is a state-of-the-art desktop video and special-effects studio. The system delivers a high-quality digital video production studio anywhere you can put a computer. It features full-screen, full-motion video capabilities — without pixel doubling. And it contains everything a developer needs to quickly and easily capture, display, edit, and output professional-quality video on videotape. It also provides professional-quality stereo sound-mixing and editing capabilities.

This bundled Apple-designed solution is built around the high-performance Macintosh Quadra 950 computer, and includes:

- Radius VideoVision Studio video capture card

- Digidesign's Audiomedia 11 16-bit sound

- Storage Dimensions MacinStor SpeedArray 2-gigabyte array

- AppleDesign Powered Speakers

- AppleCD 300 double-speed external CD-ROM drive

- Adobe Premiere Deluxe CD-ROM edition

- Radius VideoFusion

Titles and Applications

Current multimedia technology relies primarily on CD-ROM players to deliver multimedia products. These products can be developed for a wide variety of different market segments, such as home, business, or education. Each of the areas for which multimedia products are developed have their own unique applications. For example, in a business setting, a training or reference multimedia product could lake the form of an electronic performance support system used on the shop floor. In an education environment, a similar technology could be used for curriculum delivery.

Titles

Multimedia titles can be either "commercial" CD-ROMs that are sold or published in the home, business, or education market, or "in-house" CD-ROMs that are distributed within an organization.

Titles for Macintosh computers span the range from interactive shopping titles to entertainment and reference titles for the home market and clip media and market information titles used by business professionals.

Kiosks

Multimedia-based kiosks can take any number of forms. Stand-alone kiosks can have all information stored on a local CD-ROM drive, or the kiosk can be connected to an on-line network with a server containing data which must be updated on an up-to-the-minute basis.

Hybrid kiosks are those that use CD-ROMs to locally store media-rich data and link to on-line systems for delivering text-centric data.

Specific examples of kiosk usage include retail sales support; interactive museum exhibits for greater access to the museum's holdings, and medical information distribution.

Training, Reference, and Presentations

Faster access to information and increased productivity are some of the key benefits to employing CD-ROM technology in media-rich presentations. The use of CD-ROM technology in training and reference has many applications, including business field repair, customer support, manufacturing work instructions, and sales training.

Using CD-ROM for advanced delivery systems cuts across all subject areas in the education markets, for both K-12 and higher education. Examples of training and reference products in the education market include: a high school where QuickTime and other multimedia technologies are used to teach non-English-speaking students; a major university where communication between students, teachers, and administration is greatly improved by placing interactive electronic publications on the school network; and an elementary school where an archival database helps teachers provide new ways to assess students and fine-tune teaching techniques.

Desktop Video and Postproduction

As business and education users enhance their communications with video, they increasingly look to Macintosh desktop systems to provide easy-to-use multimedia solutions. The Apple Video Production System we just discussed is an example of an integrated solution.

In the corporate video and postproduction market, Macintosh computers are being effectively used as "off-line" digital nonlinear editing systems — a function previously performed by expensive, proprietary, off-line computer systems. By using Macintosh systems for postproduction, video professionals can enjoy the benefits of reduced time spent on expensive "on-line" suites, the facilitation of greater creativity in the postproduction process, and a simultaneous reduction in project costs.

Videoconferencing

As collaborative media-rich technology improves, videoconferencing continues to show promise as a high-growth area. The ultimate benefits for videoconferencing are reduced travel time and increased corporate efficiency.

A Peek into the Future

The New Media field is expanding at a rapid pace, and will continue to grow exponentially in the years to come. The promise of interactive television, of new communication technologies, of improved video and audio technologies, and the convergence of many industries will make the future of New Media an exciting one.

Apple innovations have sparked the growth of many facets of the multimedia industry and inspired the development of hundreds of new and innovative third-party hardware and software products. As part of this aggressive multimedia strategy, Apple has established the New Media Group to focus on, Apple's multimedia efforts and help develop new market opportunities for Macintosh multimedia technologies. The New Media Group provides complete multimedia solutions for the business, education, and consumer markets. It also provides continued support to the developer community to determine New Media areas that lend themselves to research and investment.

The Future of Multimedia Authoring

A Cross-Platform Standard for Interactive Media

The goal of all multimedia developers is to develop a title or application once, and then deliver this content on multiple platforms. Apple and third-party partners have started to make this goal a reality, and are continuing to introduce products that facilitate cross-platform multimedia delivery solutions.

An integral part of this cross-platform development is the ScriptX object-oriented development framework for interactive multimedia development and the Kaleida Media Player products created by Kaleida Labs.

Media Player and ScriptX from Kaleida Labs

To ensure cross-platform multimedia product development and delivery, Kaleida Labs plans to introduce the Kaleida Platform, consisting of the Kaleida Media Player and ScriptX language and development framework.

In essence, ScriptX performs the same function for interactive media as did the PostScript language from Adobe Systems for text and graphic images, providing a universal language that can be virtually device-independent. The Media Player and ScriptX work in tandem to allow low-cost development of innovative multimedia products and portable distribution of these products across platforms, using an advanced object-oriented language.

For developers, the ScriptX development framework offers an advanced object-oriented framework specifically designed for interactive multimedia applications.

For consumers, the Kaleida Media Player provides an ideal interactive software-based multimedia system that will be available on most popular personal computers. Users can display and play all multimedia data types in an integrated audiovisual presentation.

Multimedia Authoring in the Future

It is clear that the market for digital publishing tools is in its infancy and will grow rapidly throughout the next decade.

With the development of the Apple Media Kit, Apple introduced the concept of different tools for different people: designers and nontechnical content producers having one set of tools and programmers having another.

In the future, in order to serve the multitude of vertical markets, publishers will be able to create unique tool sets customized for their own publishing and production requirements. The tools will include media authoring tools and publishing tools from Apple and from third-party producers.

Along with increased tool customization, there will be improved extendability and integration between the designer and programmer tools. These changes in the type of tools available will allow designers to easily incorporate specialized objects or routines into their projects, without needing to turn to programmers to write new codes each time.

The Future of Multimedia Communications

Media-rich data will greatly increase the network bandwidth requirements in the future. The increase in the scope and depth of data transmission will mean that new protocols and enabling technologies will be required to transport data not only locally, using technology such as FireWire between devices, but also between media servers, across local area networks and wide area networks, and between high-bandwidth applications such as those used for video-conferencing and other collaborative applications.

MovieTalk

Apple is committed to providing enabling technology for media-rich data file transfer over networks. MovieTalk is a software architecture — a significant multimedia enabling technology — focused on the real-time data stream protocols required for media-rich applications such as data collaboration and video-conferencing.

MovieTalk, based on QuickTime technology, is fundamentally different from other videoconferencing schemes. MovieTalk is the only scalable network-independent and CODEC (compression/decompression)-independent solution for real-time collaboration that allows multimedia data to be distributed over networks. The MovieTalk architecture can support a variety of protocol solutions, including, but not limited to, the H-320 standard.

Since MovieTalk architecture is designed to be network-, CODEC-, and protocol-independent, MovieTalk can foster interpretability between videoconferencing and other collaboration solutions from the many third-party vendors designing New Media solutions in the future.

The Future of Television

As telecommunication and cable companies offer greater bandwidth for distributing video and audio data, there will be a shift away from CD-ROM as a delivery and storage medium to a more distributed development, delivery, and storage architecture similar to today's client-server architectures.

It is expected that "intelligent" television will soon deliver the interactive services of home shopping, video on demand, and distance learning. These media-rich services will evolve from the text-centric on-line services such as Internet and Apple's own eWorld.

Whether the device to deliver these services in the future will be a computer with television capabilities or a computer-based set-top box is still to be determined. Apple has, however, begun a number of initiatives to explore the different possibilities.

Apple released an experimental product, called Macintosh TV, a product that combines an Apple Macintosh personal computer, a cable-ready 14-inch color television and double-speed audio CD player for high-quality stereo sound into one compact, low-priced unit. Designed for users at home and in higher education institutions, Mac TV greatly reduces the cost and space requirements currently required to obtain these electronic components separately.

Later Apple announced a trial with Oracle Systems to test a Macintosh derivative set-top box for delivering interactive content, using QuickTime as the enabling technology. Apple also tested its technology model in collaboration with British Telecom in the United Kingdom. Since Apple Computer's QuickTime technology is the delivery vehicle for interactive television, developers who use QuickTime will be able to protect their investment in content on these new platforms.

Apple Multimedia Wrap-Up

Apple Computer has shown its commitment to the multimedia industry by creating the New Media division within Apple. This commitment to the research and development of New Media technologies will continue long into the future.

As part of this continuing support of New Media technologies, tools, and titles, Apple has developed a broad range of products and support strategies for the New Media market. This chapter has described Apple's current product and technology offerings, and has pointed to some of the areas where future growth and technological development will occur.

Apple is a multimedia leader, and the advantages of the Macintosh for development and delivery ensure that the Macintosh will remain a preferred platform for many New Media developers.

- The Macintosh offers ease of use through integration of hardware and software.

- Apple provides advanced media technology and tools.

- The Macintosh enables media-rich development and cross-platform delivery.

The surge in the use of multimedia by consumers is possible because the products and technologies are available now, and people from all walks of life are discovering the ways that multimedia can enhance the way they work, learn, play, and communicate.

Producing Professional Quality Sound

Audio production has been revolutionized. Now a professional recording studio on a desktop is a reality, and you can access this new digital power to add professional sound to your multimedia presentations. Working from your desktop you can create CD-quality multitrack audio productions that rival what was once possible only in a multimillion-dollar professional recording studio (Fig. 8.1).

Photo Curtesy of Turtle Beach Systems

Figure 8.1   Desktop recording studio.

If you want to produce a kiosk presentation that explains a product or service with continuous music and voice-over, or if you want to add music, sound effects, and voice to a self-paced interactive presentation, this chapter is for you.

When you build your presentation it is essential that each of its elements is complete and ready to drop in. Every authorware package discussed in this book allows you to integrate sound into the presentation. This chapter shows you how to produce high-quality sound, ready to drop into your presentation to add greater emotional impact, motivation, and excitement.

In This Chapter

In this chapter we'll take you on a step-by-step behind-the-scenes tour of a typical digital audio recording session — one that you can do at your desktop. You'll see how easy it is to work with digital sound, learn about the software and hardware needed to turn your PC or Macintosh computer into a desktop recording studio, and gain valuable recording techniques to make your productions truly professional.

Before digital audio, professional recordings were made on multitrack reel-to-reel audiotape. As each audio track was layered onto the tape, the quality of the mix decreased. The fidelity of even the most sophisticated tape is still not as high as the fidelity you can now produce at your desktop! When you record using digital technology, you layer and mix an unlimited number of tracks without adding noise or losing quality, and you gain editing flexibility that is virtually impossible using older audiotape methods. Working on your PC, with the tools you'll learn about in this chapter, you'll be able to automatically adjust the levels and balance of each stereo track, precisely cut and replace sections of audio, synchronize your audio precisely to video productions, and add magical effects that add excitement to your presentations.

Working with digitized sound is used by most contemporary producers because it:

- Allows you to perform precise editing and mixing

- Offers extremely high fidelity reproduction

- Avoids standard audiotape noise generation playback problems

- Allows you to make as many copies of the sound and as many mixes as you want without any degradation

Before moving on let's take a quick look at digital audio processing so you have a good foundation for your work in this domain.

Converting Analog Sound to Digital Sound

The audio you hear coming out of your speaker or headset is made up of analog sine waves that have a frequency in the human hearing range — typically between 20 Hz (20 cycles) and 17 kHz (17,000 cycles).

- The higher the frequency of the sine wave, the higher the tone or pitch of the sound.

- The higher the amplitude of the sine wave, the louder the sound.

Take a look at Fig. 8.1. The top portion of the figure is a close-up of an audio signal. Below this is an actual complex wave audio signal made up of thousands of sine waves of different amplitudes and frequencies. The "Actual Audio Signal" picture was taken from the editing window of one of the sound tools you'll learn about in this chapter.

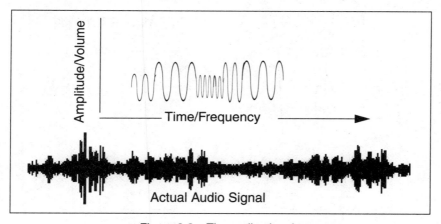

Figure 8.2   The audio signal.

The audio signals shown in Fig. 8.2 are analog amplitude/frequency signals. Computers operate in the digital word of simple 1s and 0s. Before you can manipulate sound at your desktop each audio sine wave must be converted into digital terms that your computer can understand. When you've finished editing the digital sounds, they have to be converted back to analog audio so you can hear your creation on your speaker or headset. The electronic devices that allow your computer to do this are the *digital-to-analog converter* (D-to-A) (Fig. 8.3) and the *analog-to-digital converter* (A-to-D).

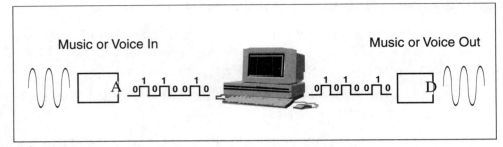

Figure 8.3   Digital/analog conversion.

The sampling process used to convert analog sound to digital sound is very straight-forward, as shown in Fig. 8.4.

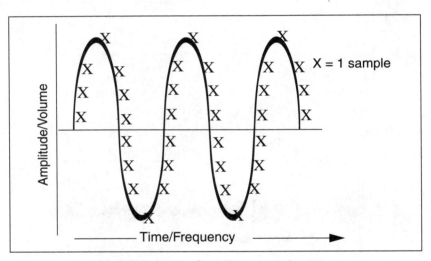

Figure 8.4   Sampling a sound wave.

Each discrete sample point is converted into a digital number and stored in the computer's memory or on a storage device. These digital numbers describe the waveform. The digital representation of the original audio signal becomes more accurate as more samples are taken, and less accurate and more grainy as fewer samples are taken. The number of waveform samples taken per second is called the *sample rate*.

The higher sample rate yields a more accurate representation of the original audio and, ultimately, a higher-fidelity recording. There is one drawback. The higher the sample rate per second, the more disk storage space is needed. Thirty seconds of single-channel (monaural) 16-bit sound recorded at a sampling rate of 44.1 kHz requires a whopping 4.5 megabytes of storage space!

Compact disks (CDs) store audio sampled at a rate of 44.1 kHz to allow frequencies up to 22.05 kHz to be recorded accurately. Because most people hear sounds only in the 20 Hz to 17 kHz range, this sampling rate generally offers more than enough audio clarity and fidelity.

Using the tools you'll learn about in this chapter, you'll be able to record sounds at the CD rate of 44.1 kHz, at the digital audio tape (DAT) frequency range of 48 kHz, and at 22.050 kHz — a good low disk-space choice for multimedia presentations that don't require superhigh-fidelity sound. In fact, except for the most discerning ear, most people won't be able to tell the difference between 44.1 and 22.05 kHz sample rate recorded sound.

8- versus 16-Bit Recording

In addition to different sampling rates, one last consideration goes into the quality of your recording — the resolution of each sample. Each sample point is represented by a digital number, and you can elect to have it represented by an 8- or a 16-bit digital number. You typically choose either an 8- or 16-bit sample number representation, based on the capability of the hardware you are using to digitize and convert your sound. The default setting on Apple's Audio Visual computer is 16-bit sound, and most sound cards for PC process at a 16-bit rate. A 16-bit rate offers virtually the highest resolution possible. An 8-bit rate provides a resolution accuracy of 0.4%, while a 16-bit number delivers 0.002% accuracy — finer than most commercially available D-to-A converters can process.

When deciding whether to record using an 8- or 16-bit setting, remember to take into consideration the equipment that is going to be used to play back the presentation. Because of its lower resolution, 8-bit sound is grainier than 16-bit sound and should be used only when you don't have the hardware available to record or play back in 16-bit sound.

A Word About MIDI

An introduction to digital sound isn't complete without a word about MIDI, which stands for Musical Instrument Digital Interface. MIDI is the standard protocol for interchanging musical information between musical instruments, synthesizers (electronic keyboards), and soundboards. *Protocol* as used here simply means a text-based language that defines instrument sounds, notes, and musical timing. You can look at MIDI as a notation (like the perforated paper rolls once used to control a player piano) that contains all the information needed to tell MIDI-equipped electronic devices which notes to play and which sounds to make (Fig. 8.5).

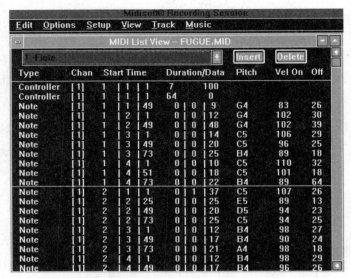

Figure 8.5   MIDI notation (from Midisoft STUDIO).

MIDI Sequencers

Top-notch MIDI sequencing software that allows you to compose and apply music to multimedia applications is now available for both PC and Apple Macintosh computers. Typical of the higher end of this genre of program is Midisoft STUDIO for Windows, which automatically places each note of your composition on your screen and records its MIDI notation as you play from any MIDI-equipped instrument. Then it allows you to edit and manipulate each note and instrument and fine-tune your composition before adding it to your presentation. The full version of this package also lets you print out sheet music that contains multi-instrument arrangements in standard musical notation. (Lower-capability versions of STUDIO are bundled with other software packages and with some soundboards.) Midisoft STUDIO also offers three views of your music to give you the depth needed to do a really professional job.

- <u>Studio View</u> lets you control the sound of your music while auditioning one, all, or selected tracks.

- <u>Score View</u> displays notes on the screen while recording your exact performance (Fig. 8.6). You can enter, edit, and watch notes highlight as the music is played back.

- MIDI List View lets you fine-tune your music by manipulating every attribute of each note. You see the changes reflected instantly in the Score View.

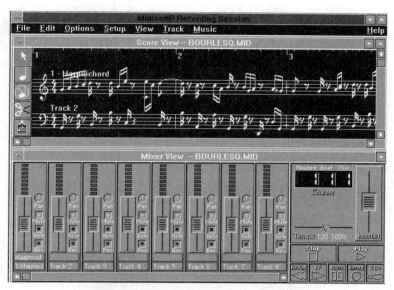

Figure 8.6   Midisoft STUDIO Score View.

FM and Wavetable Synthesis

You can buy a separate soundboard for your PC or Macintosh, or buy a "multimedia" computer with built-in sound capability. Today's soundboards and built-in capability typically include a synthesizer capable of accepting MIDI notation and playing, through attached speakers, complex compositions composed of up to 24 simultaneous voices or instruments. *The great thing about using MIDI music as a backdrop behind your presentations, or combining it with a voice-over, is that MIDI notation uses hardly any disk space at all.* It just contains the instructions in text format - all the work is done by the soundboard's synthesizer.

Today's soundboards come equipped with one of two types of musical synthesizers built in:

1. FM synthesis: Reproduces specific sounds by combining multiple sine waves to create a more complex waveform. By controlling the pitch and envelope characteristics of these

sine waves, the sounds of acoustic instruments and effects are approximated.

2. <u>Wavetable Synthesis</u>: Reproduces specific musical sounds based on actual digital recordings of each specific instrument. Wavetable synthesizers have a ROM (read-only memory) chip that contains actual studio digitally recorded instrumental sounds. The entire range of each instrument is mathematically extrapolated from the recording of each instrument, achieving an extremely realistic rendition of an actual performance.

Selecting Sound Equipment

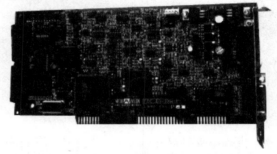

When selecting a soundboard or shopping for a computer with built-in sound, take into consideration all capabilities. It should be capable of 16-bit recording use and playback, be compatible with today's most popular entertainment and educational software packages, and deliver the MIDI sound that you need for your presentations while staying within your budget.

To give you a feeling for what you get when you make your sound investment, we've included specifications and the primary features of two standard soundboards: Creative Labs' (FM synthesis) *Sound Blaster 16* and Orchid Technology's (wavetable synthesis) *SoundWave 32*. You can use these two minireviews to familiarize yourself with soundboard terminology and specifications.

For true studio-quality recording with outputs to digital audio tape (DAT), consider doing your production work on an Apple Macintosh II or Quadra series computer using a high-end board from a vendor like Digidesign, Inc., who supply full 16-bit stereo 48-kHz recording with digital output. Abbreviated information about Digidesign's professional and home recording studio equipment is included later in this chapter.

If you have an Apple Macintosh AV series computer, or are planning to purchase one, and if you don't need DAT output, and you want to do high-end quality productions, consider using DECK II AV software from OSC, or the upgraded version of Sound Edit Pro from Macromind • Paracomp, Inc. Both of these software packages work <u>without</u> a soundboard by taking advantage of the Macintosh AV's built-in digital signal processor (DSP) to edit and manipulate sound for your presentations. Both sound editors are excellent. Each has its own strengths and weaknesses, and you might consider owning both to get the benefit of Sound Edit's special effects and DECK II AV's advanced studio mixing and editing capabilities. An overview of both of these software packages is presented later in this chapter along with reviews of a number of Microsoft Windows-compatible audio editing packages.

A Typical Desktop Audio Production

This section walks through a typical desktop audio production to give you a feel for the process and help you become acquainted with audio terminology and the capabilities of digital recording. The examples and screen shots you'll see are from OSC's DECK II AV software. I used this software package to illustrate digital recording because it contains all the elements used by the professionals, and allows me to show you some of the advanced techniques and concepts not available on all audio software packages. (You can choose from many audio software packages for both the IBM PC and compatibles and Apple Macintosh computers, as you'll discover later in this chapter.)

What You'll Need

To produce audio for your presentations you should have:

- Either an IBM or compatible PC or an Apple Macintosh computer

  - Built-in CD ROM recommended

  - PCs equipped with a soundboard or built-in sound chip (DSP) digital signal processor

  - Apple Macintosh AV with built-in DSP (no soundboard needed) or other Macintosh II, Quadra, or later computers with a soundboard

- Inexpensive audio mixer

- High-quality microphones

- Stereo headset

- Cassette or reel-to reel tape deck

- Stereo tuner/amplifier with multiple inputs and outputs

- Sound-editing software

- Optional MIDI interface

    - MIDI software

    - Synthesizer or keyboard

A Digital Workstation — Putting All the Pieces Together

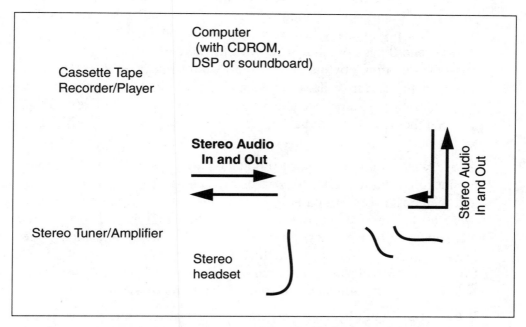

Figure 8.7   *Typical desktop recording studio configuration.*

My basic configuration includes a Macintosh Centris 660AV computer with built-in CD-ROM and a digital signal processor (DSP), and a simple mixer that allows me to mix to and from my cassette tape deck, listen to the mix on my headset, and put down voice tracks with my two microphones (Fig. 8.7). Most of the latest Power Macintosh computers come equipped with a digital signal processor, and have the speed and flexibility that makes them excellent sound-production workstations. INTEL Pentium®-equipped PCs also have the speed and power to put you light-years ahead of even the most sophisticated studio of just a few years ago.

The Audio Production Script

Once you have assembled and connected your hardware and chosen the audio editing software and become familiar with it, you should write the audio script that's going to accompany your visual presentation. An audio script can include narration, actors (the actors can even be synthesized robot voices), sound effects, and music, all timed to work with your presentation. Because an audio production is complex, you must have a written script before you begin the recording session. See Chap. 4 and 5, *"Interactive Presentations"* and *"Presentations"* for template examples and helpful techniques.

When you are adding sound to a self-running presentation, or an interactive presentation that includes long segments of narrated action, record the narration with a high-quality tape recorder while watching the on-screen action. Before recording, you should dry-run the screen action with the script, and fine-tune the timing by making on-the-fly adjustments to the presentation, the script, or the narrative pace before making the final cut. Once you have the timed narration on tape, use it as an audio input to one of the recording tracks. You can then add musical background and sound effects to polish the presentation.

As we walk through a typical production, we'll use scene 1 from a script I produced on digital audio for one of my clients. It is much like a radio play, and includes actors, sound effects, and music. I've chosen this short scripted scene as an example because it exercises almost all the necessary production elements you'll use when you mix your first audio. The final three-scene product was 10 minutes in length and took 10 hours of in-studio production time. It began with the actors reading the script, followed by a complex mix where timing was adjusted and sound effects and music were added.

If the script hadn't been as well crafted as it was, we could have conceivably spent twice as much time in the studio, and studio time is expensive! *Assemble all the elements and be well prepared before you begin the production process.* You'll save valuable time and the result will be truly professional.

The Recording Session

On-Screen Studio Tools

Today's on-screen audio studio tools mimic the look and feel of mixers with additional controls and surfaces. If you have ever seen or used a multitrack recording deck you'll feel comfortable with today's on-screen metaphors. If this is your first time working with audio, you'll find that all the audio production software packages for Windows and the Macintosh are intuitive and easy to use. Figure 8.8 shows DECK II AV's Mixer and Transport window.

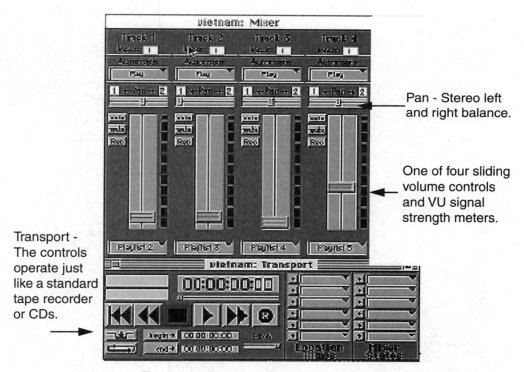

Pan - Stereo left and right balance.

One of four sliding volume controls and VU signal strength meters.

Transport - The controls operate just like a standard tape recorder or CDs.

Figure 8.8   Mixer board and transport controls.

The Mixer has four vertical input/output modules. Each module is complete with sliding volume control, a pan (stereo left/right balance) control, and a VU meter that dynamically displays signal level. Each input/output module controls the volume and pan of each of four digital record/playback tracks. (DECK II AV allows you to create an unlimited number of tracks, but only four of those tracks play at one time.) Each input/output module has two modes — <u>record</u> and <u>play</u>. Record lets you feed an audio signal into your computer for processing, set its monitor level, and digitally records it to your hard disk. Once a track is recorded, play mode lets you play back the track while manually or automatically adjusting its volume and pan.

The controls in the Transport window operate just like a standard cassette player/recorder, with a tape-counter readout, and controls that let you rewind, fast-forward, play, stop, and record each digital track. The Transport window also lets you store location times, punch time, mixer states, and adjust playback pitch. We'll get into the details of most of these features as we use the tool during an actual recording session later in this chapter.

The Waveform Editor rounds out DECK II AV's suite of audio tools. The Waveform Editor (not available in nondigital audio studios) brings the power of digital audio editing to your desktop. With it you can manipulate audio signals, adjust their timing, and perform "nondestructive" edits that are impractical and often impossible using older analog techniques. The DECK II AV tool never erases existing audio as you make edits. This nondestructive feature allows you to revert to previous versions to recover from a mistake or change your mind. The Waveform Editor contains many other sophisticated features, such as volume and pan automation, playlist architecture, and more that we'll explore during the recording session (Fig. 8.9).

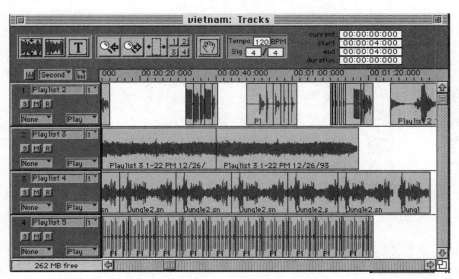

Figure 8.9   DECK II AV's Waveform Editor.

Using a Waveform Editor is very much like using a text editor. You can highlight portions of sound, cut them out to the clipboard, paste them back anywhere on the page, pick up and move sound bits from track to track or anywhere along a track's timeline, go in for a close magnified look, modify a specific portion of the wave shape to add special effects, and much, much more. If you are at all familiar with today's word processing programs, you'll find working with digital audio a snap.

The Recording Sequence

In an ideal world the audio production process follows this sequence:

1. Record the first track on track 1.
2. Play back track 1 to make sure you like it, and set the volume.
3. Record track 2 while listening to track 1.
4. Play back both tracks while recording track 3.
5. Follow this same procedure to record track 4.

Once you have "laid in" all your tracks, you listen and mix the levels and set the pan for all four tracks. (You can add an unlimited number of tracks by bouncing all four tracks into one, leaving room to add three more tracks and do even more bouncing/track combining.) You can automate the volume and pan settings at this time. When you are satisfied with the sound of your composition, you save this "master" as a digital file. You would then export this sound file directly into your presentation, link it to an event in your presentation, export it as analog audio sound to a cassette tape or, if you are using a high-end soundboard, export it in digital audio tape (DAT) format for pressing a CD or album.

The Session

Now that you've had a quick tour of the equipment and software, and overviewed a sequence you can use when making your recordings, let's jump in and do an actual session.

A traditional session is broken into two parts; production and postproduction. During production we record all the material. In postproduction, we blend it all together to achieve the final product. In this session, the line between production and post production phases was blurred because we were trying out different sounds and ideas along the way. Don't worry about following a specific production formula. Be flexible - the quality of the final product is what counts.

Tip Some computers put out excessive fan noise that could reduce the quality of your recording. To lessen the impact of this noise put foam windshields over your microphones, move as far away from the noise source as possible and, if necessary, build a noise shield out of a cardboard box lined with soundproofing tiles. I've known some people who found the noise so intrusive that they actually cut a window in an inside wall and set up a shielded studio in the adjacent room.

Here's scene 1 from the audio production script. You'll discover as we convert the script into a "living" production that some of the effects aren't the same as originally written. They were changed during production to enhance the work, or because the original concept wasn't feasible. Creativity and inventiveness often jump in during the production phase, making the final product better than you could have ever imagined when you conceived it. But the importance of up-front planning cannot be overemphasized. Without it, there would be no guide, story line, or the chance for improvement.

SCENE I

Light music-in, fading to sound of crickets, then rooster crowing, then

WIZARD
Booming Voice

[Fade in slowly]

Jake, Jake wake up, a new dawn is rising. It's time to get designed in for '93!

JAKE

[Fade in as if coming out of a dream]

What? What? Huh . . . ?

WIFE

Honey, wake up. It's getting late. You're going to miss your flight!

JAKE

But, I thought I heard someone say "get designed in for '93." Was that you?

WIFE

You must have been dreaming.

JAKE

But it seemed so real, so immediate . . . It's getting late, I'd better get moving if I'm going to make my flight.

[Transitional music]

JAKE

[*Sound of strapping himself in*] I'm going to get above the competition for a bird's eye view.

[Short rocket launch sequence 3, 2, 1, blast-off, fading into outer space beep-beep Sputnik sounds]

Producing Scene I

Since we were working with four active tracks we decided to use track 1 for Jake and his wife, track 2 for the Wizard, and tracks 3 and 4 for the sound effects and music. (Newer versions of DECK II offer six active tracks.)

We first recorded Jake and his wife on track 1 by checking and setting our microphone record levels on the external and computer screens' mixers. To begin, we pressed the track 1 record button in the Waveform Editor, then pressed the Transporter's play and record buttons (Fig. 8.10). We named this segment "Jake/Wife Scene I," and then recorded the Wizard's one-line introduction on track 2 and named it "Wizard Scene I."

Tip Because we used very sensitive microphones that picked up the slightest hint of noise, the actors had to be extremely careful when they turned their scripts over. To minimize the sound of turning pages we put the script's pages in a stack, and as the actors finished each page they slid it off carefully.

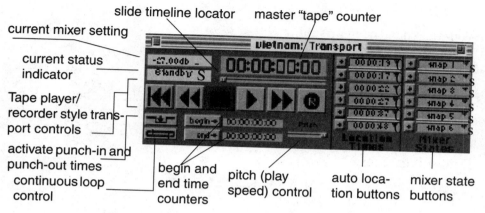

Figure 8.10   *Annotated DECK II AV Transport controls.*

When we played back the Wizard's part we didn't feel that it was strong enough, and decided at this point to enhance it by making multiple copies of his speech, putting each copy in its own track, and offsetting each track by 0.1 second. When we played back all four tracks, the Wizard sounded powerful and almost menacing. We then *bounced* the four tracks together and placed the resultant mix in track 2.

Bouncing tracks is one of the most powerful features of this, and other, waveform editors. When you "bounce" tracks you essentially mix them together in the background, remove the original tracks from the editor's screen, and then place the resultant mix anywhere you want to on the editor. With DECK II AV the bounce is "nondestructive." This means that the original information (even though it no longer appears on the screen) is saved on your hard disk - just in case you want to go back to it. Because we're operating in the digital domain, you can bounce literally hundreds of tracks together without any degradation in the quality of the sound. You don't introduce any noise or distortion and the result is crystal clear.

Once we were satisfied with the narrative portion of the production, we aligned the Wizard's short speech to flow directly into Jake's first words. Finally, it was time to do the fun part, adding the sound effects and music.

Sound Effects and Music

The script called for the sound of crickets, followed by a rooster crowing, fading into the Wizard's booming voice. We have two excellent sound effect CDs that contain hundreds of effects and sounds. The *SoundBank* from Turtle

Beach Systems comes packaged with their Turtle Tools audio software package, and we also have a *Hollywood Edge* demonstration disk that comes packaged with Digital Soup's software. Between these two disks, and the complete *Hollywood Edge* sound effects CD, you can find almost any sound you need. The operative word being "almost." Although there is a cricket sequence, there is no crowing rooster. We had to make do with what we had, and elected to begin the scene with a chirping nightingale flowing into a gently rolling harp crescendo. We recorded these onto tracks 3 and 4 directly from the computer's built-in internal CD-ROM drive.

DECK II AV doesn't offer an easy way to create an echo (other programs for Windows and for the Macintosh, such as *Soundedit Pro* from Maromind, do - albeit at 22 kHz/8 bits), so we decided to automatically fade into Jake's first sentence. Doing this using DECK II AV is simple and straightforward. All we had to do was select a fade-in shape and apply it to the waveform. The shape begins at zero volume and increases gradually to full volume. We could have also elected to draw in our own custom fade rather than using DECK II AV's default shapes. Figure 8.11 shows what a fade-in looks like on the Waveform Editor:

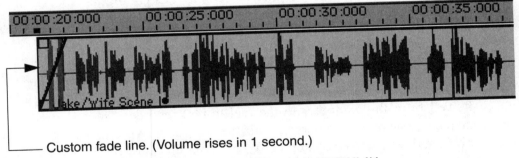

Custom fade line. (Volume rises in 1 second.)

Figure 8.11   Automatic fades in DECK II AV.

With this tool, we could have also added automatic pan by drawing a line over the waveform. When the line is at the top of the waveform, the sound comes from the left speaker, and when it is at the bottom of the waveform, the sound comes from the right speaker. I used these automatic features in another production to make a stationary helicopter sound appear as if it were approaching from the left, getting nearer (increased volume), hovering above us, and receding to the right by decreasing the volume line and moving the pan line to the bottom of the waveform. Using DECK II AV you have the option of programming volume and pan directly into the mix, or doing this manually during playback (Figs. 8.12 and 8.13).

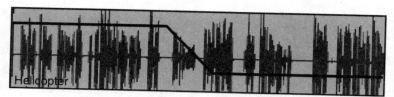

Figure 8.12   Automated pan from left to right.

Figure 8.13   Automated volume from low to high to low.

The Final Mix and Mastering

Once all the actors, sound effects, and special effects were laid down digitally, it was time for the final mix. This production was going to be used as a sales training aid, so we elected to master our production to a high-quality-studio reel-to-reel tape rather than directly to a CD or digital tape. (If this production were going to be distributed on CD we would have taken the digital route.) The reel-to-reel tape was ultimately used as the master to run off 2000 cassette tapes.

With earphone on and the script in front of him, the audio engineer made slight, last-minute volume and fade adjustments as the final production flowed from the computer to the reel-to-reel recorder. He corrected for tiny nuances that most listeners wouldn't even know existed, but that he recognized and wanted to clean up before he'd put his name on the production.

Once you do this enough, you too may become a perfectionist, cleaning up minute pops, hisses, and adjusting the volume "just right." It all comes with doing. And with today's tools the doing can be an exciting adventure of sound exploration that leads to outstanding professional results.

Sound Equipment and Software Overviews

The State of the Art Is Moving Fast

Software and hardware developers are not standing idle while I write this book, and by the time this book is published all of the products introduced here will be enhanced and improved. They will have friendlier user interfaces, operate more efficiently, and have more bells and whistles. But they will all retain their basic underlying operating characteristics and capabilities.

These minireviews will give you a good feel for what to expect from each product, and help you decide which products, or product types, are best suited to your audio production needs.

In This Section

This section provides basic features and specifications for a number of PC and Apple Macintosh sound software and hardware products, and is divided into two subsections: one for the PC and one for Apple Macintosh-related products.

PC Products

Hardware

- Sound Blaster 16 (Creative Labs)
    - FM synthesis 16-bit soundboard
- SoundWave 32 (Orchid Technology)
    - Wavetable synthesis 16-bit soundboard

Software

- Audio View (Voyetra Technologies)
    - Digital Audio Wave Editor, Mixer, CD-ROM Controller
- Sound Impression (Midisoft)
    - Complete digital audio tool set and player environment
- Wave for Windows (Turtle Beach Systems)
    - PC Recording Studio
- The Turtle Tools (Turtle Beach Systems)

- Complete digital audio tool set with MIDI, and player environment
- Sound Professional (Digital Soup)
- PC Recording Studio
- Midisoft Studio (Midisoft)
    - MIDI Sequencing and Authoring Software
- MusiClips (Voyetra Technologies)
    - Multimedia MIDI song file collection
- Multimedia Music Library (Midisoft)
    - Multimedia MIDI song file collection

Apple Macintosh Products

Hardware

- Digidesign
    - Complete hardware/software audio solutions for Apple Macintosh Computers

Software

- DECK II and DECK II AV (OSC Media Products)
    - Macintosh Recording Studio
- MacRecorder Sound System Pro (Macromind/Paracomp)
    - Macintosh Recording Studio
- Metro (OSC Media Products)
    - Synchronized MIDI sequencing for Macintosh

PC Audio Hardware: Typical Features and Specifications

<u>Product Name:</u> **Sound Blaster 16**

<u>Manufacturer</u>: **Creative Labs, Inc.**
1901 McCarthy Blvd.
Milpitas, CA 95035
(408) 428-6600

<u>Overview</u>: Sound Blaster 16 is a mid-range 16-bit soundboard for PC computers. Provides FM music synthesis, based on a Yamaha OPL3 FM synthesis chip.

<u>System Requirements (minimum)</u>

- IBM PC, AT, or 100% compatible

- Minimum 640 KB RAM

- MS-DOS 3.0 or higher

- EGA or VGA (recommended)

- Speakers or headphones

<u>Specifications and Features</u>

- True 16-bit CD-quality stereo sound

  - 16- and 8-bit stereo playback/recording

  - Autodynamic filtering

  - Selectable sampling rates from 54 Hz to 44.1 kHz

  - 90-dB, 16-bit CODEC DAT chip

- Software-based audio compression system

  - capable of handling 16-bit, 44.1-kHz stereo files

  - Supports ADPCM, CCITT, A-Law, and u-Law standards

- Four-operator, Two-voice stereo music FM synthesis

  - OPL3 (Yamaha) FM Synthesis chip

  - Power-on default to Sound Blaster-compatible mode

- Stereo digital mixer

  - Full software control of fade-in, volume, left/right steering, and microphone mixing

  - <u>Output mixing sources</u>: Microphone, CD-audio, line-in, FM music, digitized voice and PC speaker-in

  - <u>Input mixing sources</u>: Microphone, CD-audio, line-in, and FM music

- MIDI interface

  - Compatible with MPU-401 UART and Sound Blaster modes

  - Optional MIDI adapter hardware and software

- CD-ROM interface

  - Supports optional high-performance internal or external CD-ROM drives from Creative Labs, or models CR521, CR523 from Panasonic

- Microphone automatic gain control (AGC) Amplifier

  - Selectable AGC with 600 ohms input impedance and 10- to 200-mV sensitivity

  - Microphone included

- Joystick port

  - Standard PC joystick port for 1 or 2 joysticks (Optional Y-cable)

- Output power amplifier

  - 4 W per channel (PMPO) at 4-ohm minimum load impedance.

  - Mini stereo jack to RCA conversion cable included

- Controls

  - Volume, bass and treble, and input/output gain control

<u>Bundled Software</u>: The board ships with a starter kit of software that lets you exercise its capabilities. Bundled software includes an assortment of sound utilities, a CD Multimedia Encyclopedia, plus:

- Creative Wavestudio™

  - Windows-based, full-featured wave editor software that supports MIDI and drag-and-drop capability. It allows multiple source recording and direct mixer control. Editing features include cut and paste, echo, fade, amplification, and reverse.

- Creative Mosaic™

  - A demonstration game that includes sound effects.

- Creative Soundo'le™

  - A sound-recording utility that allows you to record from multiple sources in 16-bit format with compression.

- Creative Talking Scheduler™

  - A programmable talking scheduler that verbally reminds you of scheduled events.

- HSC Interactive™ (Special Edition)

  - Multimedia authoring software including animation and image enhancement.

- PC Animate Plus™

  - Animation and special-effects studio.

- Monolog for Windows™

  - Add speech to virtually any windows application.

(The above listed software is Trademarked by Creative Labs, Inc.)

Product Name: **SoundWave 32**

Manufacturer: **Orchid Technology**
45365 Northport Loop West
Fremont, CA 94538
(510) 683-0300

Overview: SoundWave 32 is a full-featured soundboard that uses wavetable synthesis to accurately reproduce music and sound effects. Wavetable synthesis is FM synthesis based on actual recorded sounds. For example, a synthesized piano sound is derived from a root recording of a piano's notes. (FM synthesis and wavetable synthesis are defined earlier in this chapter.)

System Requirements (minimum)

- IBM PC, AT, or 100% compatible

- Minimum 640 KB RAM

- MS-DOS 3.0 or higher

- EGA or VGA (recommended)

- Speakers or headphones

Specifications and Features

- Audio

  - Wavetable synthesis

  - 16-bit sound

  - Line output

  - Home audio interface cables

- Business

  - Windows sound system compatibility

  - Voice annotation (microphone is included)

- Multiple simultaneous sound standard compatibility

  - SoundBlaster+

- General MIDI
- Sound Blaster+ Roland MT-32
- WSS + Roland MT32
- WSS + General MIDI

- Game
  - Roland MT-32 sound module
  - SoundBlaster compatibility
  - MIDI and Joystick ports
  - CD-ROM Interface

- Interface
  - Mic IN, Line IN, Line OUT
  - MIDI IN and OUT
  - Joystick IN
  - Speaker OUT
  - CD-Audio IN
  - CD-Interface (Mitsumi and Sony)

- Multimedia
  - Supports General MIDI Synthesizer, MPU-401, MT32, SoundBlaster, and MPC (Multimedia PC) Level II.

PC Audio Software

Product Name: **AudioView**

Manufacturer: **Voyetra Technologies**
5 Odell Plaza
Yonkers, NY 10701-1406

(914) 966-0600

Description: Digital audio wave editor, mixer, and CD-ROM controller (Fig. 8.14).

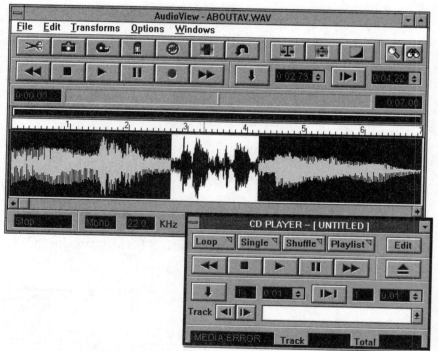

Figure 8.14   Voyetra AudioView and CD-ROM controller.

System Requirements (minimum)

- A Multimedia PC and Microsoft Windows with Multimedia Extensions, or

- IBM PC or 100% compatible with windows 3.0, or 3.1 and most soundboards.

Specifications and Features: AudioView creates an image of the digital audio signal in a Multimedia PC or PC sound card and gives you total control over the sound you hear. It offers recording studio options that allow you to:

- Mix multiple audio files, such as voice, music, and sound effects with full volume control.

- Use industry standard sound files in *.WAV or *.VOC format, in both mono and stereo.

- Tailor sound files to any application with comprehensive editing features such as cut, paste, trim, silence, and scale.

- Enhance sounds with echo, fade, reverse, and other custom effects.

- Convert bit resolutions and sample rates to play digital audio files on a wide variety of hardware.

- Monitor record and playback levels with a dynamic stereo VU meter.

- Zoom in to view and modify sounds at the finest resolution.

- Link and embed sounds using Microsoft Windows 3.1 Object Linking and Embedding (OLE).

In addition, an audio mixer control utility controls input and output signals on a Multimedia PC's audio mixer hardware from a panel of slide controls on your PC screen. A CD-ROM audio player utility provides a front end to control audio tracks on a CD-ROM drive, making it easy to select a track range, create custom playlists, name tracks, and log CD titles.

Product Name: **Sound Impression**

Manufacturer: **Midisoft Corporation**
P.O. Box 1000
Bellevue, WA 98009

(206) 881-7176

Description: Digital audio wave recording and editing, mixer, CD, MIDI and WAVE player configured as a virtual "rack-mounted" stereo player (Fig. 8.15).

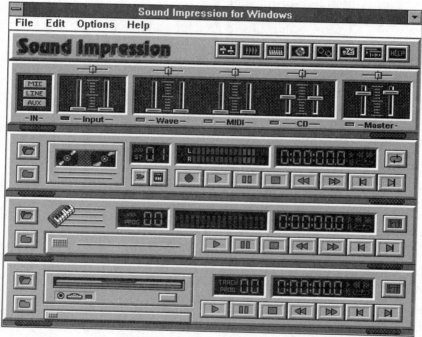

Figure 8.15   Sound Impression's virtual rack-mounted stereo system.

System Requirements (minimum)

- Microsoft Windows 3.1

- DOS 3.1 or higher

- 386-based PC

- 4 MB RAM

- On floppy disk drive, and a hard disk drive with 4 MB of free space

- Sound card with Windows Multimedia drivers installed

- EGA or VGA monitor

- Mouse or other pointing device

- CD-ROM drive (optional) with Windows Multimedia drivers

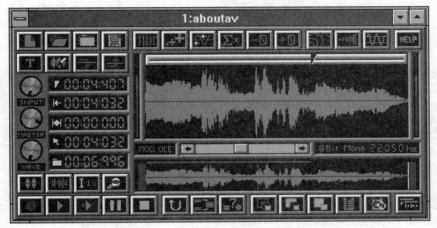

Figure 8.16   Sound Impression's Wave Editor.

<u>Specifications and Features</u>: Sound Impression is a complete audio recording and playback studio featuring virtual "rack-mounted" components that look and feel like your stereo system. This tool provides professional-level Wave recording, editing, and mixing capabilities, OLE server support for WAVE, MIDI, and CD sound (Fig 8.16). Sound Impression's features include:

- 16 wave editing sessions (multiple track recording)

- Hard disk recording

- 16-track wave composer

- OLE-compliant server

- Special effects tools

- Multiple sound card support

- Comprehensive on-line help

Product Name: **WAVE for Windows**

Manufacturer: **Turtle Beach Systems**
52 Grumbacher Rd., Ste. 6
York, PA 17402

(717) 767-0200, (800) 645-5640

Description: Full-featured personal recording studio. Reshape the music you create, assemble full multimedia audio presentation, even rearrange songs from your favorite discs with WAVE for Windows (Fig. 8.17).

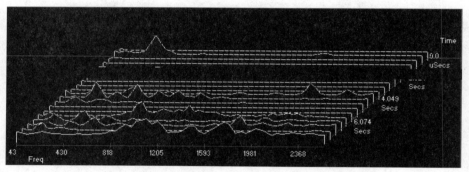

Figure 8.17 WAVE for Windows frequency analysis.

System Requirements (minimum)

- MS-DOS 3.1 or later, Windows 3.1 or later, or 3.0 with Multimedia Extensions

- Multimedia PC or equivalent (386-compatible or greater), 2 MB of RAM, 30-MB hard disk, VGA, mouse, and a sound card

- Works with any Windows 3.1-compatible sound card

Specifications and Features: Standard audio editing functions plus advanced frequency equalization and analysis tools allow you to create simple to complex audio productions (Fig. 8.18).

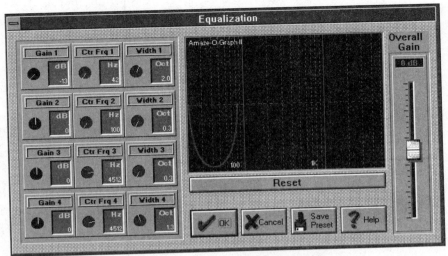

Figure 8.18 WAVE's equalization window.

WAVE for Windows' capabilities include:

- Recording with all the features of a tape recorder. Works with 8- or 16-bit mono or stereo at 11.025-, 2.05-, or 44.1-kHz sampling rates.

- Cut-and-paste editing lets you visually manipulate sound clips.

- Gain adjustment lets you change the volume of all or part of a file to create perfect fade-ins and fade-outs.

- Full undo protects you against mistakes.

- Visual analysis tools let you view your sound in several different ways. You can view and analyze sound in variable resolution windows or put your sound data into a 3D waterfall display. Displays can be calibrated in time, samples, beats, time code, or film feet and frames. All colors are user-definable.

- Waveform drawing lets you fix glitches in your sound file by selecting draw mode and drawing the wave with your mouse.

- Crossfading capability lets you smooth out a presentation when combining two different sound files. You control the length of the fade-in and -out.

- Digital equalization using WAVE's 4-band parametric equalizer lets you improve your sound by featuring desired sounds or removing unwanted ones.

- Sound mixing lets you mix up to three sound files into a fourth (bouncing) while controlling the volume and the starting time of each file.

- Time compression or expansion capability lets you change the time duration of a sound clip without affecting the pitch for perfectly timed presentations.

- You can import and export a wide variety of sound files, including .SFI, WAVE, .16, .8, and .VOC file formats. You can also change the sample rate of a file while converting it, using WAVE's true sample rate converter.

Product Name: **The Turtle Tools for Multimedia**

Manufacturer: **Turtle Beach Systems**

52 Grumbacher Rd., Ste. 6
York, PA 17402

(717) 767-0200, (800) 645-5640

Description: *The Turtle Tools for Multimedia* is a set of audio tools designed
for multimedia production work that includes the *WAVE* audio editing and
playback software, plus a version of *Midisoft Session* MIDI sequencer and
musical development software. In addition, this comprehensive bundled package also includes a *KeyPlayer* that lets nonmusicians play and record using
the PC's keyboard, *MIDI Tune-up*, a MIDI file editor for nonmusicians,
SoundBank, a CD-ROM filled with over 300 sound effects, and *SoundAttach*
software that lets you attach MIDI and/or WAV sound files to all Windows
actions.

System Requirements (minimum)

- MS-DOS 3.1 or later, Windows 3.1 or later, or 3.0 with
  Multimedia Extensions

- Multimedia PC or equivalent (386-compatible or greater), 2 MB
  of RAM, 30-MB hard disk, VGA, mouse, and a sound card

- Works with any Windows 3.1-compatible sound card

Specifications and Features: *The Turtle Tools for Multimedia* is designed
specifically to cover all your multimedia needs. Essentially, its six components include almost everything you need to take full advantage of your Windows 3.1-compatible sound card or multimedia computer.

6. WaveTools: Wave audio recording, editing, and playback
   application (Fig. 8.19).

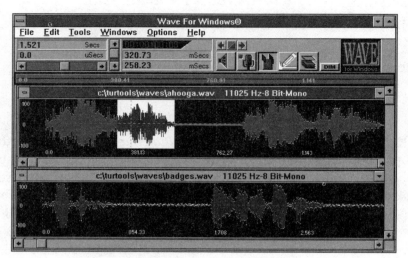

Figure 8.19 WaveTools.

7. <u>Midisoft Session</u>: MIDI sequencer for developing and editing musical compositions (Fig. 8.20). This version of this software includes all features, except the ability to print out your musical composition. (The complete version is provided by Midisoft, and is reviewed later in this chapter.)

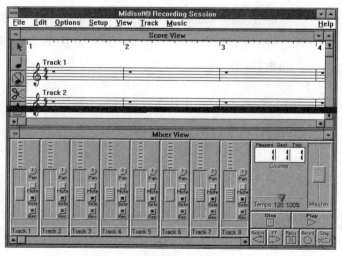

Figure 8.20 Midisoft Session.

8. <u>KeyPlayer</u>: Turn your PC's keyboard into a musical instrument (Fig. 8.21).

Figure 8.21 KeyPlayer.

9. <u>MIDI Tune-up</u>: MIDI file editor that lets you graphically
    change tempo, key, instrument, and other settings (Fig. 8.22).

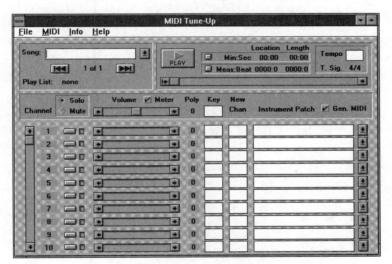

Figure 8.22 MIDI Tune-up.

10. <u>Sound Attach:</u> Allows you to attach MIDI and/or WAV
    sound files to all Windows actions (Fig. 8.23).

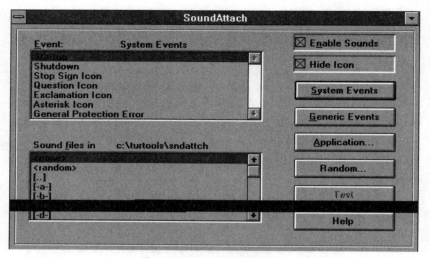

Figure 8.23 Sound Attach.

11. <u>SoundBank CD-ROM</u>: This CD-ROM contains over 300 sound effects and musical pieces in four different WAVE formats, and in Redbook professional-quality audio. These effects can be used on a PC or Macintosh computer equipped with CD-ROM drive.

Product Name: **Digital Soup Sound Professional**

Manufacturer: **Digital Soup, Inc**.
P.O. Box 1340
Brattleboro, VT 05302
(802) 254-7356

Description: *Digital Soup Sound Professional* is a multitrack recording studio with an intuitive tool bar that gives you instant access to a complete audio tool kit. The tool bar has descriptive icons and context-sensitive help that make it easy to learn and use. Sound Professional's advanced functions include a Power Spectrum display for analysis, and frequency equalization that allows you to shape your audio response.

The package comes with a sample CD-ROM from Hollywood Edge that includes almost 100 sound effects and music clips you can use in your productions. Digital Soup also distributes the complete Hollywood Edge series of CDs, which includes more than 1500 sound effects in this 20-MB collection (Figs. 8.24 and 8.25).

Figure 8.24 Digital Soup's Track Editor.

System Requirements (minimum)

- MS-DOS 3.1 or later, Windows 3.1 or later
- Multimedia PC or equivalent (386-compatible or greater), 2 MB of RAM, 30-MB hard disk, VGA, mouse, and a soundboard
- At least 5 MB of free hard disk space is also recommended

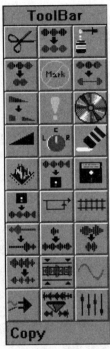

Figure 8.25 Digital Soup's ToolBar.

Features: *Digital Soup Sound Professional* offers these features for your multimedia sound-editing needs:

- Access professionally produced sound clips. An audio CD with nearly 100 sound clips is included.
- Work with 8- or 16-bit sound at 11, 22, and 44 kHz.
- Mix voice, music, and sound effects on up to 16 tracks.
- Preserve original waveforms with nondestructive editing.
- Experiment with effects quickly, using formula-based editing.

- Cut and copy a segment of sound, and paste in any of three modes: cover, insert, or mix.

- Stereo-lock two tracks and edit them simultaneously and they remain synchronized.

- Apply a wide variety of sound effects: modulation, compression, sound reversal, repeat, delay, and others.

- Use variable-cure panning and leveling capabilities.

- Clean up unwanted characteristics with frequency filters.

- See the frequency content of your sound with spectral analysis.

- Change the length of your sound to fit the time requirements of your multimedia project, without affecting pitch.

- Use OLE (Object Linking and Embedding) to create true multimedia documents.

Product Name: **Midisoft Studio**

Manufacturer: **Midisoft Corporation**
P.O. Box 1000
Bellevue, WA 98009

(206) 881-7176

Description: *Midisoft Studio* is a MIDI sequencing program that shows your exact musical performance instantly on the screen as standard music notation. It allows you to fine-tune your music with powerful editing features and see the results appear on a musical staff. The software offers three views:

1. *Studio View* and tape deck buttons: Control the sound of your music. Audition one, all, or selected tracks; overdub.
2. *Score View*: See notes appear on the screen while recording. Enter, edit, and watch notes highlighted as you play back your music (Fig. 8.26).
3. *MIDI List View*: Fine-tune your music by manipulating every attribute of each note. See the changes reflected instantly in Score View.

Midisoft Studio allows you to compose, record, play, save, and print musical scores for a variety of applications, including stage and dance performances, business presentations, trade show music, and more.

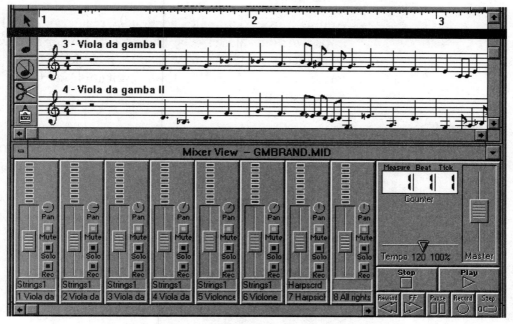

Figure 8.26 Midisoft Studio Score View.

System Requirements (minimum)

- IBM PC/Compatible, 286+, 2 MB (386+, 4 MB recommended)

- Microsoft Windows 3.1 with Mouse

- Windows-supported sound card or MIDI interface (for playback)

- MIDI musical instrument (optional)

Suggested Applications

- Performers/rehearsal

  - Use during rehearsals to play many instruments simultaneously when the whole band can't be present, or practice alone with the software playing other parts.

- Music education

  - Enhances appreciation and understanding of music by allowing you to watch notes highlighted as you hear the song. See how key signatures, time signatures, and familiar rhythm patterns look when notated.

- Business and Multimedia

  - Adding music to graphics generates greater emotional impact to your sales efforts. This program, when used with Multimedia Windows or Midisoft's included DLL, integrates music into Windows applications and presentations.

Features:

- Standard notation appears on screen instantly in real time during recording, editing, and playback. Notes are highlighted during playback.

- Enter and edit notes directly on the score with a mouse. Instrument-playing skills are not required.

- Cut, copy, and paste notes, phrases, and complex passages.

- Record up to 32,000 tracks, limited only by computer memory.

- Stop Record/Stop Play to enter and review complicated passages one note at a time.

- Record and edit all types of MIDI data, including controller and pitch bend and program changes.

- MIDI Sync can connect to SMPTE, FSK, and other standard interfaces.

- Multiports can access 32+ MIDI channels.

- Mixer view allows point-and-click control of loudness, pan, mute, solo, and instrument assignment.

- Note resolution up to 64th notes and triplets is included.

- Context-sensitive help is available.

Macintosh Audio Hardware

Many of today's Macintosh computers include a digital signal processor (DSP) that processes stereo sound in real time. With this built-in capability, the need for plug-in soundboards has diminished. However, high-end boards and software are needed for studio productions where the output must be digital (for mastering a CD, for example). In addition, sound processing boards can enhance and expand the Macintosh computer's built-in capabilities.

Digidesign offers the broadest selection of Apple Macintosh-compatible boards and software of any vendor. They provide complete audio system packages, including hardware and software to meet virtually any requirement:

- Home studio system
- Project studio system
- Film/video postproduction studio system
- Professional recording system
- Broadcast production studio system

If you are interested in home or business studio production using the latest model Macintosh computers, contact:

Digidesign
1360 Willow Road
Menlo Park, CA 94025

(800) 333-2137, (415) 688-0600

Macintosh Audio Software

Three products, from two vendors, are featured in this section to give you a feel for the capabilities offered for Macintosh sound production. As with the PC products, we used these audio products to add sound to actual multimedia projects.

Product Names: **DECK II and DECK II AV**

Manufacturer: **OSC**
2901 23rd Street
San Francisco, CA 94110

(415) 252-0460

Description: Professional studio-quality 16-bit audio processing software with full QuickTime movie and synchronization support.

DECK II System Requirements and Support

- Apple Macintosh IIX, CX, CI, VX, LCII/III, Quadra, Performa 400/600, or Centris 650 with hard disk and 4 MB of RAM

- System 7.1 or higher

- QuickTime 1.5 or higher (included)

- Supports a full range of Digidesign's sound/NuBus audio cards

DECK II AV System Requirements

- Apple Macintosh AV (Audio Visual) computers

- System 7.1 or higher

- QuickTime 1.5 or higher (included)

About DECK II (AV) Features: DECK II and DECK II AV are top-of-the line professional recording software packages used by a high-end user base. The DECK II software is used in professional studios with Digidesign's wide range of audio cards. The DECK II AV is ideal for business or home production using Apple's series of AV (Audio Visual) computers. Many of the features listed here are written for the professional user. Call or write OSC for product information that meets your needs. Flip back to the short tutorial at the beginning of this chapter to see DECK II AV in action!

Recording Features

- 16-bit linear digital multitrack hard disk recording

- 4.1- and 48-kHz sample rates

- Six tracks

- Ability to record to multiple destination disks

- Virtual tracks for unlimited playlists

- Nondestructive recording and overdubs

- Scrub from disk

- Automated punch in and out

- Loop/rehearse mode

Editing Features

- Multitrack visual waveform editing (Fig. 8.27).

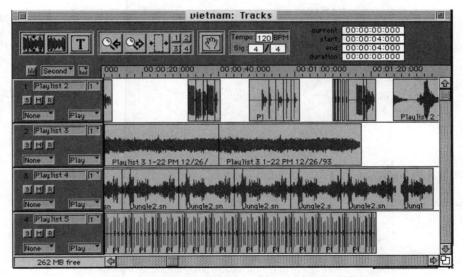

Figure 8.27 DECK II (AV) multitrack visual editing.

- Nondestructive track and region slip

- Edit and spot to time code or bar/beat

- Nonmodal region editing

- Constructive fades and crossfades

- Reverse, invert, normalize, and batch-normalize regions

- Mix to clipboard

- Grid support with full nudging

- Fully implemented undo

- Record directly into the waveform display (Fig. 8.28)

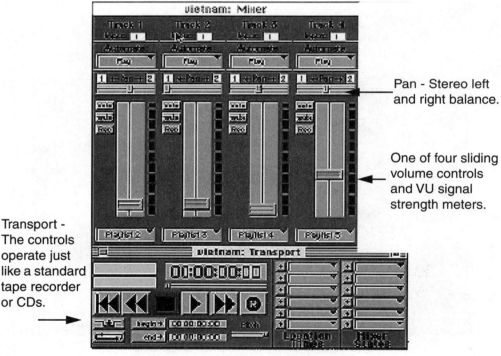

Pan - Stereo left and right balance.

One of four sliding volume controls and VU signal strength meters.

Transport - The controls operate just like a standard tape recorder or CDs.

Figure 8.28 DECK II (AV) Mixer and Transport.

Automation and Mixing Features

- 24-bit moving fader automation
- Automate with mouse or external faders
- Visual editing of automation data
- Copy and paste automation envelopes
- Automated mix to disk
- Automated mix to digital output (DECK II only)
- Unlimited constructive track bounce

QuickTime Features

- Audio synchronized to QuickTime movies in a window
- Scrub QuickTime picture with audio chase
- QuickTime movie scrubs when audio regions are placed
- Mix audio to 8- or 16-bit QuickTime files

Synchronization Features

- Supports all SMPTE time-code rates, including 29.97
- True continuous slaved resynchronization on playback
- Supports film-to-video pulldown rates with no additional hardware (44,056 and 48,952 Hz)
- Captures current frame
- Reads and generates MIDI time code and beat clock

Product Name: **METRO**

Manufacturer: **OSC**
2901 23rd Street
San Francisco, CA 94110

(415) 252-0460

Description: Full-featured MIDI sequencing application for the Macintosh that provides all the record, compositional, and real-time editing capability needed to produce professional projects.

METRO runs in tandem with OCS's DECK II and DECK II AV multitrack recording and editing software, allowing you to add MIDI music to your mix.

QuickTime movie postproduction capabilities allow you to accurately place MIDI music to accompany your video productions.

METRO Requirements and Support

- Apple Macintosh computer with 1 MHz of RAM or more with Apple sound chip

- System 6.07 or higher

- Supports QuickTime and operates in the Open Music System™ (OMS™) environment which allows all OMS-compatible application to gather information about your studio setup.

Recording Features

- Two loop recording modes

- Internal and external metronome with accents

- Punch in and overdub

- MIDI input filtering

- Step recording

Editing Features (Fig. 8.29)

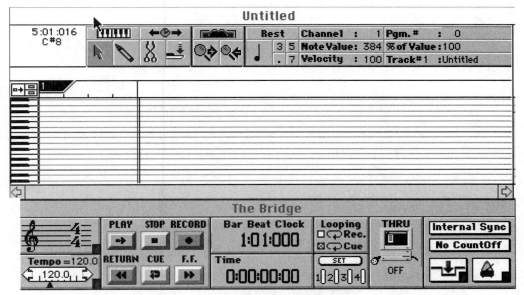

Figure 8.29 METRO editing tool set.

- Transpose, reverse, harmonize in scales or chromatically, human feel, quantize, compress, and expand in time

- 32 sections, 99 tracks per section

- 16 subsections per track with 99 tracks per subsection

- Undo and redo

- Graphic editing of continuous data, including tempo and velocity

- Tab markers

- Standard MIDI import and export

- Graphic real-time MIDI data editing

- Selection filter for editing operations

- Extract program names from SYSEX

- Velocity stems editing

- Multiple track views in note editor

- Multiple paste with optional transpose

- SYSEX and scale creation and editing

- Auto create instruments

Automatic and Control Features

- 254 instruments (>255 MIDI channels with OMS) and 8 layers

- Auto moving fader assignable to any controller

- Group instruments faders with polarity for fades and crossfades (Fig. 8.30)

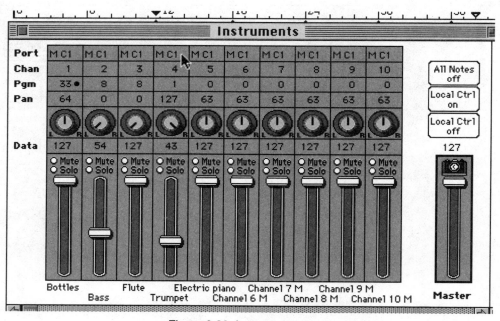

Figure 8.30 Instrument control.

- Chase controllers and program changes

- Variable parts per quarter note

- Multiple time and key signatures

- SMPTE or bars display in editor windows

- Tap tempo tool and MIDI monitor display

- Remote control of transports, step record, and controllers

- MIDI list even editor
- Scrubbing in not editor and list editor
- Snapshot instruments when recording
- Looping for entire track/multiple loops within a track
- Gapless cue looping for precise editing – four cue/selection points

Synchronization Features

- Clock: MTC, song pointer, internal
- MIDI time-code support (SMPTE)
- Multiple timing options: extended time manager
- Sync to DEC II or DEC II AV on a single Macintosh computer

Product Name: **MacRecorder Sound System Pro**
(*Includes MacRecorder and Sound Edit Pro*)

Manufacturer: **MacroMind – Paracomp, Inc.**
600 Townsend
San Francisco, CA 94103

(415) 442-0200

Description: MacRecorder Sound System Pro is an audio software and hardware workshop that lets you record, edit, and play back live or recorded sound on your Macintosh. Use the MacRecorder Sound System Pro to enhance multimedia presentations, training materials, and documents with voice and music.

Hardware: The package comes with *MacRecorder* digitizer and built-in microphone for use with non-AV Macintosh computers. This hardware interface is plugged into the printer or modem port of your Macintosh.

Software: *SoundEdit Pro* sound, editing software allows you to record, edit and mix voice, music, and sound effects. You use this software with the MacRecorder on non-AV Macintosh computers, and directly with AV computers. *SoundEdit Pro* can record directly to disk, and edit or play from disk, so the length of sound is not constrained by available memory. Sound appears on the screen as a waveform for easy editing. Cut and paste just like text. You can modify sound with special effects such as backward, echo, reverb; and you filter whole selections or selected portions of your sound.

SoundEdit Pro lets you mix multiple music tracks, sound effects, and voice to produce multitrack sound tracks. You can also choose sampling rates or compression ratios to control memory usage.

Requirements and Support

- Apple Macintosh computer with 68020 processor or greater, system 6.07, 2 MB RAM, System 7 or later, 4 MB RAM

- Two MacRecorders to record in stereo (or use Sound Edit 2 on a Macintosh AV computer to record and play back in stereo without using the MacRecorder hardware)

Features and Specifications

MacRecorder (*needed with non-AV Macintosh computers*)

- Sample 8-bit size at rates up to 22 kHz

- Built-in microphone with input level control and line-input and mic-input miniphone jacks

SoundEdit Pro (Fig. 8.31)

- Record, edit, and play to and from disk

- Input with any device whose driver is Macintosh Sound Input Manager-compatible

- Open and save 8- and 16-bit sample sizes at rates up to 48 kHz

- Multitrack mixer for mixing multitrack sound files into stereo or mono

- Compress sound at ratios of 3:1 to 8:1

- Spectrum view in 2D or 3D for visualizing sound frequencies

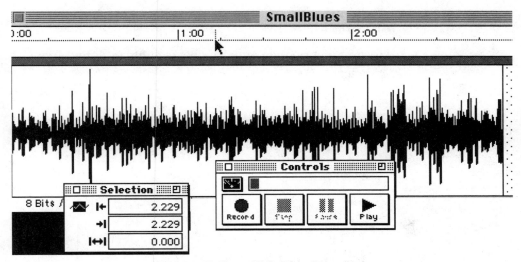

Figure 8.31 SoundEdit Pro editing display.

<u>File Formats opened and saved</u>

- SoundDesigner II, SoundEdit, SoundEdit Pro, Systems 6 and 7 sound resources, AIFF-C

<u>Effects include</u>

- Amplify, backward, bender, echo, envelope, filter, flanger, loopback, reverb, tempo
- Record stereo with two MacRecorders or by using a Macintosh AV-series computer

<u>Compatible products</u>

- MacroMind Director

- MacroMind MediaMaker

- MacroMind – Paracomp Magic

- QuickPICS

- HyperCard

- QuickMail

- Microsoft Mail

- Any application that supports the Macintosh Sound Input Manager

Sound Effects and Music Clips

Adding sound effects and music enhances your audio presentation. The following resource listing is a good cross section of available sources.

CD-ROM Sound Effects and Music

Turtle Beach Systems
52 Grumbacher Rd., Ste. 6
York, PA 17402

(717) 767-0200, (800) 645-5640

- SoundBank Audio Collection

Prosonus
11126 Weddington Street
North Hollywood, CA 91601

(800) 999-6191

- SampleCell Volume 2

- Sound Ideas Sound Effects Library

East-West Communications
302 Ocean View Avenue
Del Mar, CA 92014

(800) 833-8339

- ProSamples Series

Optical Media International
180 Knowles Drive
Los Gatos, CA 95030

(800) 347-2664

- Sonic Images & Master Studio Libraries

OSC
2901 23rd Street
San Francisco, CA 94110

(415) 252-0460

- A poke in the ear with a sharp stick (parts 1 and 2): noninstrumental sounds

GREYTSOUNDS
(818) 773-7327

- Volume 1: SampleCell

McGill University

(514) 398-4548

- Master samples classical sounds

Invision

(408) 438-5530

- Percussion and synthesized sounds

The Hollywood Edge

From Digital Soup at (800) 793-7356, or by calling (800) 292-3755

- The Hollywood Edge sound effects library

MIDI Music Clips

The following MIDI music clip libraries are published for the IBM PC or compatible computer. However, if you order them on a 3.5-inch floppy, they can be used on a Power Macintosh, or on a Macintosh computer that accepts and translates PC information.

Midisoft Corporation
P.O. Box 1000
Bellevue, WA 98009

(206) 881-7176

- Multimedia Music Library: MIDI song files for multimedia production

Voyetra Technologies
5 Odell Plaza
Yonkers, NY 10701-1406

(914) 966-0600

- MusiClips: MIDI song files for multimedia production

PC Soundboard Resource List

Table 8.1 lists IBM PC and compatible 16-bit soundboard manufacturers and their phone numbers so you can call and request product information. (*Please keep in mind that most major IBM PC and compatible computer manufacturers. such as IBM, Compaq, and AST, are producing computers with built-in sound digital signal processors. The effect of this trend is to reduce the need for stand-alone plug-in soundboards.*)

TABLE 8.1   PC Soundboard Vendors

16-bit PC Soundcard vendor	Telephone number
DSP Solutions	(916) 621-1787
Focus Information Systems	(510) 657-2845
Genoa system	(408) 432-9090
Jovian Logic	510-651-4823
Logitech	(800) 231-7717
MediaMagic	(800) 624-8659
Media Resources	(714) 256-5048
Media Vision	(800) 845-5870

TABLE 8.1   PC Soundboard Vendors

16-bit PC Soundcard vendor	Telephone number
Microsoft	(800) 426-9400
MIDI Land	(909) 595-0708
Multiwave Innovation	(415) 875-7602
Omni Labs	(800) 706-3342
Orchid Technology	(800) 767-2443
Roland	(213) 685-5141
Sceptre Technologies	(714) 993-9193
Sigma Designs	(800) 845-8086
Sun Moon Star	(408) 452-1411
Tecmar	(216) 349-0600
Turtle Beach Systems	(800) 645-5640
Wearnes Technology Group	(408) 456-8838
Zoltrix	(510) 657-1188

Digital Video – A New Creative Frontier

Animations, still graphics, or sound, by themselves, are all good ways to communicate the value of your product or service. But when you add video, complete with synchronized sound, to your presentation you bring the viewer into your world for an intimate visit. Video is a familiar medium, and brings with it a sense of comfort that can enhance your presentation's creditability. Figure 9.1 shows how easy it is to work at home or in a small office when producing professional video for your presentations.

Photo Courtesy of RasterOps

Figure 9.1   Home video production

In this chapter you'll see how easy it is to put together the equipment and software needed to do a splendid job of video production, right in <u>your</u> own home or office, plus we'll walk you through a basic video production to give you a feeling for the tools and techniques you can use when crafting your video productions.

In Figure 9.2, a doctor explains the effects of a drug to other doctors in a friendly one-to-one way that brings a human touch to a very technical topic.

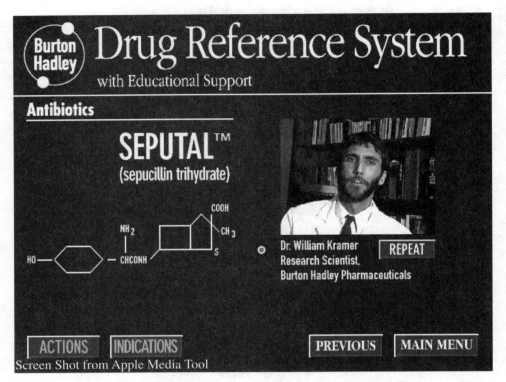

Figure 9.2   Doctor explains antibiotic use — Apple Media Tool.

Video mixed into a multimedia presentation is an extremely effective teaching tool that can show a process, a place, or give the viewer a front seat to any of the worlds that video offers.

Today, using advanced video compression schemes like those in Apple Computer's latest QuickTime software release, you are not limited to postage-stamp-sized video windows you can produce full-screen video that delivers the same impact as up-close-and-personal television. (*Learn more about QuickTime in Chap. 7, and read about Windows and video in Chap. 6.*)

Video Does Have Some Drawbacks

- <u>The ability to view your presentation.</u> Today, not everyone to whom you send video is able to view it at its best resolution. Video boards that increase the screen's effective resolution must be added to standard PCs to display a clear crisp video image. However, the proliferation and easy availability of multimedia PCs portends that soon virtually every PC will have full video capability. Know your audience and their capabilities to take advantage of video production before using it in your presentations.

- <u>Large File Size.</u> The second drawback is storage. Video, even when it's compressed, requires enormous amounts of disk space 10 seconds of compressed video can use as much as 1 megabyte of storage. This means that approximately 6 megabytes of storage space is needed for every minute of video — and that's before you add synchronized sound. With sound, you're looking at storage approaching 10 megabytes per minute. This may limit your distribution methods to CD-ROM or direct network transfer for networked presentations.

Digital video is a must for many business presentations, even with these minor technical considerations. You can mold and shape the content of digital video in creative ways that were never possible before, and the fact that you can do it all on a desktop computer makes working with digital video refreshing and exciting. The results are astounding, and can make any presentation stand out and deliver your message loud and clear.

Video Jargon

Here's a short list of some of the acronyms and specifications you'll hear bandied about when you read and talk about digital video.

- <u>AVI (Audio Video Interleaved)</u>

    Audio Video Interleaved is Microsoft's software technology for playing full-motion video sequences on PCs that support Windows capabilities. You can use AVI to create presentations, display digital video sequences, display animation sequences, and present multimedia slide shows. The term *interleaved* refers to the way video and audio data are alternately stored in a video file.

Many video boards come bundled with Microsoft's *Video for Windows* software that facilitates AVI.

- Frame

  The basic unit of information in television, video, and AVI movies; a single image or field. The specifications for frames vary according to the television format used.

- NTSC (National Television Standards Committee)

  The U.S. television standards organization. The NTSC format for transmitting television and video specifies a frame rate of 30 frames per second and a frame size of 640 6 480 pixels.

- PAL (Phase Alternate Line)

  A format for transmitting television and video that is used in more than 60 countries. The format specifies a frame rate of 25 frames per second and a frame size of 768 6 576 pixels.

- SECAM (Sequential Color and Memory)

  A format for transmitting television and video used in France.

Working with Digital Video

Video, like a traditional motion picture, is made up of a series of photographs (called *frames*) each showing an animated progression. Standard video, however, stores and processes these images in analog fashion. Playing a videocassette on your VCR is similar to playing a music tape on your cassette player. In both cases the information is stored on magnetic tape as changes in amplitude and frequency, and then sent directly to the video or audio equipment where you watch and hear it. Digital video, like digital audio described in detail in Chap. 8, is made up of a series of digital 1s and 0s. This allows each bit of video information be manipulated by a computer, giving you control over images that just isn't possible in the analog domain.

With digital video you can change the sequence of frames by simply clicking on a frame and moving it on your computer's screen; you can change the color, shape, and virtually anything on any individual frame or group of frames; you can add and synchronize audio narration, music, and sound effects; and then, when you're finished, you can export the entire production as an analog signal that can be saved on standard videotape and played on a standard TV or monitor.

You'll Need Some Video Hardware First

Before you run out and buy video software to process your images, you have to have a way to get the video you took using your camcorder into your computer for processing. Many multimedia PCs come with video boards built in. These boards convert the analog video and sound signals from a video player into the digital 1s and 0s that your computer understands.

Video Boards for the PC

If you don't buy a PC with built-in video hardware, you can buy capture boards that are easy to install and come with all the software you need to begin doing basic video processing. As an example, MediaVision offers its Pro MovieStudio video capture board, with real-time compression, that comes with everything needed to capture and compress digital video from your camcorder, VCR, laser disk, or any other NTSC, PAL, or SECAM source. Using Pro MovieStudio, you compress video in real time, so it plays back at either 30 frames per second in a 160 6 120 pixel window or at 15 frames per second in a larger 320 6 240 pixel. This board, like most others for the PC, comes bundled with software that lets you step right into video production.

VideoSpigot for Windows, produced by SuperMac Technology, is distributed by Creative Technology, Ltd. (the same people who manufacture Sound-Blaster) and provides an easy plug-in way to add video power to your PC. This video board also comes complete with all the software you need to jump into video production.

Figure 9.3   High-end video boards for your PC.

For high-end productions, where you need professional studio-quality results using your PC, check into products from Truevision (a RasterOps Company) (Fig. 9.3). Their TARGA 2000 high-end digital video card for EISA-based PC computers supports Microsoft's *Video for Windows* software, including full-frame video playback with desktop preview and full-frame video capture. The TARGA 2000 video card records full-frame, full-motion video and audio to disk at 60 frames per second NTSC (or 50 fields per second PAL), for super-high-resolution video performance.

Video Boards for Macintosh

The Apple Macintosh AV series of computers comes equipped with built-in video capture and can output digitized video in NTSC or PAL formats so you can put your final work on videotape.

If you don't have an AV computer, you can update your existing Macintosh or Power Macintosh by adding boards by a number of manufacturers. VideoSpigot for Macintosh, for example, produced by SuperMac Technology, provides an easy plug-in way to add video power to your Macintosh. This video board also comes complete with a starter pack of video software.

RasterOps, in Santa Clara, California, offers a complete video solution, named MoviePak Presenter, designed specifically for multimedia presentation applications (Fig. 9.4). The RasterOps Presenter solution package integrates video capture technology with enhanced MoviePak software technology to bring full-motion QuickTime movie capture and playback capabilities to a 640 6 480 screen at an affordable price. It also delivers 24-bit color to a 13/14-inch Apple monitor or other compatible display.

Figure 9.4   RasterOps MoviePak solution.

The MoviePak Presenter package captures QuickTime movies, plays back movies that have been captured, and is perfect for authoring QuickTime movies for CD-ROM, interactive multimedia, video kiosk applications, business presentations, and entry-level video postproduction.

As shown in Figure 9.5, the MoviePak Presenter provides:

- RasterOps 24STV video board, enhanced MoviePak technology with integrated compression and decompression, and AVID VideoShop 2.0 software

- Support on Macintosh II, Centris, or Quadra computers

- Full compatibility with all QuickTime Applications

- 24-bit color for 13/14-inch Apple or compatible computers

- 30 frames per second full-screen video recording
- 60 frames per second full-screen playback
- JPEG compression and decompression

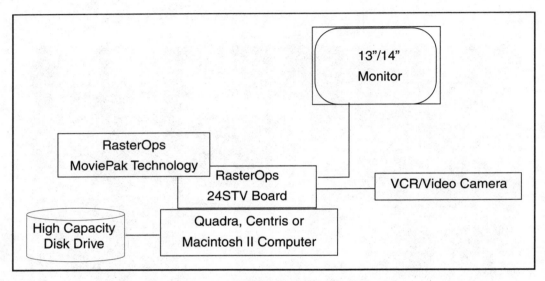

Figure 9.5   Multimedia authoring system.

Video Software

Microsoft's Video for Windows Software

Video for Windows is digital video software from Microsoft that provides the video input link from a video board into a Windows environment. It is sold stand-alone or comes bundled with many Multimedia PCs and video boards, and consists of a number of tools to help you do entry-level video production work.

VidCap

VidCap is a data-capture application that lets you capture video sequences onto your PC computer system. With VidCap, you can capture individual images or entire video sequences from a VCR, a videodisc player, or a video camera and microphone. VidCap focuses on data collection; other functions, such as editing, compressing, and formatting captured video sequences for playback are supported by the Video for Windows VidEdit tool.

VidEdit

VidEdit lets you create and edit audiovisual sequences consisting of a series of frames that contain digital audio and video data. With VidEdit, you can edit one or more frames of a video sequence and adjust the audio, video, or video-palette components of each frame.

Using VidEdit, you can add, delete, or move multimedia data in your video sequences. You can synchronize a presentation by moving sound data to match the video image. When you finish fine-tuning a video sequence, you can generate a compressed, interleaved AVI file. VidEdit lets you adjust compression parameters to allow for such factors as image quality and the data transfer rate for your particular storage device.

You can run multiple copies of VidEdit simultaneously, which is useful if you need to edit and refine portions of a sequence.

Media Player

Video for Windows includes the Media Player for playing video sequences and for adding video to presentations, spreadsheets, word processing, and other electronic documents. Media Player can play several types of media sequences, including digitally recorded sound, Musical Instrument Digital Interface (MIDI) sequences, and video sequences. It can also be used to control any Media Control Interface (MCI) multimedia device installed on your system. For example, you can use Media Player to play video sequences and digitally recorded sound files, as well as to control devices that play audio compact discs and videodiscs.

BitEdit

BitEdit is used to perform simple edits and color changes to bit-map images, and to work with the PalEdit software to edit color palettes associated with bit-map images.

With BitEdit, you can edit captured or scanned bit-maps, or you can import and enhance images from other paint programs. BitEdit supplements, rather than replaces, full-featured paint and editing programs. Although BitEdit offers some image-editing capabilities, it is usually best to invest in a more sophisticated program to create bit maps or make extensive changes to existing bit-maps.

PalEdit

PalEdit provides color touch-up capabilities for digital images. It is used to improve image quality, prepare images for display on different types of hardware, and to prepare multiple images for simultaneous display. PalEdit is used for the following:

- Modify any color in a palette.

- Modify the entire color palette for brightness, contrast, or color tint. Scanned images often require touch-up for brightness or contrast. Tinting and other special effects are also available.

- Reduce the number of colors in a palette. Managing the number of colors in a palette can save memory or improve consistency among a group of pictures. PalEdit lets you control the way colors are reduced, so you can preserve the quality of a bit map even though its palette is smaller.

- Copy colors from one palette to another. Then, combining bit-map images or creating special effects, you can copy colors from one palette to another. PalEdit allows you to use the Clipboard to copy and transfer one or more colors among palettes.

- Build a palette that works with multiple images or video sequences. Using the color-reduction and color-copying features of PalEdit, you can build a composite palette that contains the most important colors for a group of visual elements together, such as video sequence and several bit maps. You can also use PalEdit to link a composite palette back to each bit map providing the colors.

WaveEdit

WaveEdit provides basic digital sound recording and editing, and produces waveform files that you can incorporate into Windows applications, documents, and video sequences.

With WaveEdit, you can also cut unwanted or unnecessary sounds from a waveform file. Because waveform files can require large amounts of memory and storage space, you can use WaveEdit to shorten these files without removing important information. WaveEdit can also be used to create simple sound effects by repeating various parts of a waveform file, or by cutting segments from one file and pasting them to another.

Supplemental Tools

Video for Windows includes two supplemental applications called Media Browser and Video for Windows Converter. Media Browser lets you examine and play video clips from the Video for Windows CD-ROM. The Video for Windows converter lets you modify QuickTime (Apple Computer) movies to play with video for Windows.

Macintosh Video Editing Tools

The Macintosh has rapidly become the professional platform of choice for many corporate and professional video producers. The range of hardware/software packages available is staggering, and growing rapidly.

Essentially, you first have to determine how high a production quality you want to produce and then decide how much money you are willing to spend to achieve your results. If you are reading this book your needs are probably confined to getting video into a Mac and incorporating it into multimedia presentations. You may also want to create CD-ROMs — but not necessarily at full-screen quality. Meeting these needs is rather straightforward, and requires only a Macintosh computer with at least 8 MB RAM, a VCR/camcorder, a video capture card (if you don't own a Macintosh AV), and video-editing software. If you already own the computer and a high-capacity hard disk, you've already made your major investment.

A Digital Video Production

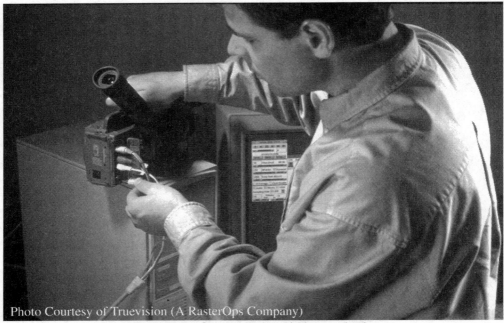

Photo Courtesy of Truevision (A RasterOps Company)

Figure 9.6   Camcorder input/video production.

The best way to really understand the power of digital video is to take a look at a simple video production process (Fig. 9.6). I elected to show you how it's done using *Adobe Premiere* because this comprehensive and powerful digital movie-making and video-production tool is available for both the Macintosh and IBM PC and compatible computers. As a bonus, I've also added a section in this chapter that shows how you might use a special-effects tool, such as VideoFusion, to add excitement and interest to your video productions. Another valuable tool for digital video and digital-still photograph production is Adobe Photoshop. You can use Photoshop to enhance individual video frames, and it's a definite must for other multimedia-related digital photo production work — look into this package! You might also consider getting a high-end graphics tool, such as Aldus IntelliDraw, to round out your production tool kit.

Adobe Premiere Basics

Adobe Premiere is a versatile video-and-audio-editing software tool that can be used by professional and novice alike. It allows you to combine source material or clips to make a movie, and then view and play the movie using any application that supports the Quicktime movie format. A final Adobe Premiere movie is a file that you create after assembling and editing clips that can include material from any of these sources:

- Digitized video captured from cameras, VCRs, or tape decks
- Quicktime movies made using Adobe Premiere or other sources
- Animations
- Scanned images or slides
- Digital audio recordings and synthesized music and sound
- Adobe Illustrator files
- Adobe Photoshop files
- FilmStrip files created in Adobe Premiere and edited in Adobe Photoshop
- Titles and backdrops

You can create your own video and audio clips by recording material to your Macintosh hard disk using a variety of hardware products.

Eight Steps to Final Production

Adobe Premiere is a powerful editing and video-composition tool, but to give you a feel for basic video production, we'll just skim through the eight essential steps needed to produce and view a successful video production. Figure 9.7 shows this process graphically.

1. Import video and audio clips onto Premiere's Project window work space.
2. Drag an audio clip from the Project window to any audio track.
3. Drag a video clip onto video track A.
4. Drag a clip to video track B. Then select the clip and apply a filter to it.
5. Drag a transition onto the track.
6. Preview the movie's composition.
7. Select Movie from the Make menu to finish the process.
8. Play your new movie by clicking on the Play button in the Clip window.

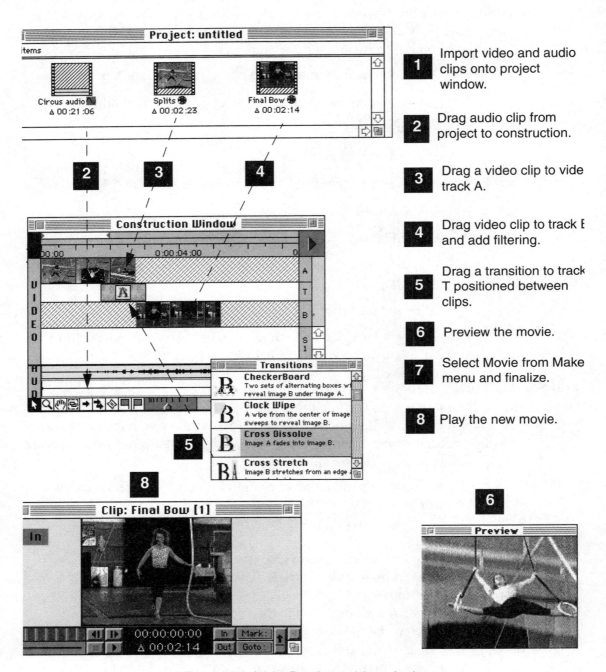

1 Import video and audio clips onto project window.

2 Drag audio clip from project to construction.

3 Drag a video clip to vide track A.

4 Drag video clip to track E and add filtering.

5 Drag a transition to track T positioned between clips.

6 Preview the movie.

7 Select Movie from Make menu and finalize.

8 Play the new movie.

Figure 9.7   Adobe Premiere quick production.

Special Effects

Adobe Premiere includes built-in transitions that allow you to elegantly move between scenes with effects like fades, wipes, and dissolving checkerboard patterns. You can also import movies from Adobe Premiere directly into Adobe Photoshop, where you can enhance and modify your work on a frame-by-frame basis. Working in Adobe Photoshop allows you to add surrealistic touches to your production, or to remove or enhance specific parts of each frame.

VideoFusion - Special, Special Effects

Another video editing and production package, VideoFusion, really lets you delve into the world of special effects with its built-in morphing capabilities and other WOW, POP, BANG features (Fig. 9.8).

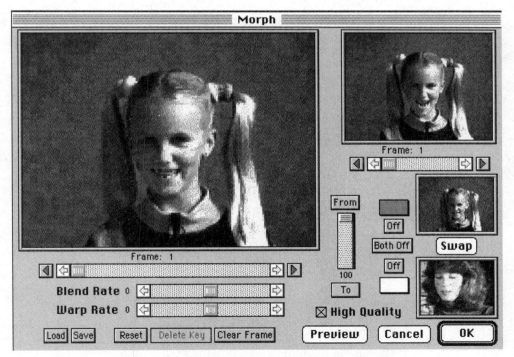

Figure 9.8   Morphing work space in VideoFusion.

The following list of special effects shows how versatile VideoFusion is:

- <u>Pan-zoom-rotate</u>

    Dynamically change the view of your movie over time to create 3D fly-by effects, picture in a picture, rotation, and zoom.

- <u>Warp</u>

    Stretch movies like a rubber sheet for fun-house mirror and liquid effects. Create powerful metamorphosis effects by combining this 2D mesh warp with movie blending.

- <u>Composite</u>

    Combine movies with a broad range of tools. VideoFusion's composite capability allows you to overlay movies, graphics, and text; it also provides extensive movie arithmetic to combine traveling mattes.

- <u>Color</u>

    Manipulate the color of your images with custom color palettes. Intensify, soften, or even change colors. Cycle colors for time-varying color changes, or rebalance them for tinting movies. Calculate color edges automatically and overlay on a movie to create hand-painted effects.

- <u>Metamorphosis</u>

    Change one image into another seamlessly by "morphing."

- <u>Direct channel processing</u>

    Commands operate directly on a selected channel instead of on the entire movie.

- <u>Key-frame-based dynamic filters</u>

    You can control filter parameters over time by setting key frames at the beginning and end of a selection. Intervening values are interpolated for you, creating dynamic changes as your movie plays.

VideoFusion provides a complete software solution for QuickTime post-production. This tool allows you to create movies with scalable technology. You can adjust movie size, frame rate, and compression to create CD-ROMs, business presentations, kiosk presentations, and training videos using JPEG compression technology and broadcast-quality video.

We've Just Scratched the Surface

Doing postproduction video work at your desktop is a reality. This chapter has presented only a few of the tools and some of the ways for manipulating video on your PC or Macintosh computer. Essentially, you have compete control over every aspect of the final video product. You can manipulate and mold it in ways that were not possible just a few years ago.

Dive in! If you already have a camcorder and a computer, all you need is a video board and a minimal amount of software to get started. Many boards are bundled with basic postproduction video software editors. These usually provide more than enough capability to allow you to grasp the possibilities and make the decision to increase capability or stick with what you have. "Lights, camera, action!"

A New Way to Deliver Your Message

KODAK Photo CD *Portfolio* technology puts high-end presentation development at your desktop, and portable presentation ease in your brief-case.[1]

Like slide presentations, Photo CD Portfolio discs that you produce on a Macintosh computer feature high-quality still images and graphics enhanced with music and narration.

The distribution disks can be played back, with the presenter in full inter-active control, on virtually any multimedia PC or Macintosh computer equipped with KODAK CD-compatible drive, or on a standard television set using a Photo CD player.

In addition to making your presentation using a photo CD player from companies like Apple Computer, 3DO/Panasonic R.E.A.L., or CD-I, KODAK offers a convenient Photo CD portable player (PCD970) that connects quickly to any TV and fits easily into any briefcase (Fig. 10.1).

---

[1]Many of the photographs used in this chapter are courtesy of Eastman KODAK Company and were entered directly into this layout from a KODAK Portfolio compact disc.

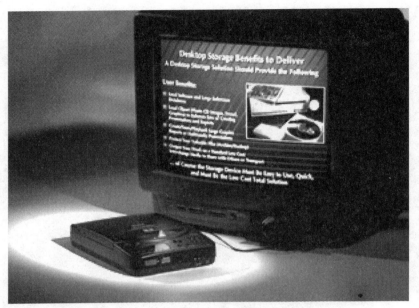

Figure 10.1   KODAK portable CD player.

Portfolio CDs Are Interactive

The finished product is an interactive CD that lets the user determine on the fly what information he or she wants to present. Because CDs can hold so much information (more than 600 MB of information), you could craft a presentation for a wide range of audiences and, during each show, use only those parts of the presentation that address a specific audience's needs.

The Software Production Tools

Figure 10.2   Create-It and Arrange-It production software.

KODAK offers three software packages that let you create Photo CD Portfolio discs (Fig. 10.2):

- <u>KODAK Create-It</u>

    - Photo CD presentation software lets you create presentations with simple, interactive menu choices and virtually unlimited options for designing individual frames.

- <u>KODAK Arrange-It</u>

    - Photo CD Portfolio layout software lets you design more advanced multimedia programs with sophisticated layouts. With Arrange-It, you can import images and frame designs from Create-It or from other applications such as Adobe Photoshop.

- <u>KODAK</u> Build-It

    - Both Create-It and Arrange-It output a script language used by Build-It to structure the images, text, sound clips, and other content onto a Photo CD Portfolio disc.

The Production Cycle

During a typical production cycle, you create your presentation using Create-It and/or Arrange-It authoring software (Fig. 10.3). You then take the output script and other material to a KODAK authorized service center that uses the Build-It software and CD-ROM mastering equipment to produce your finished Portfolio CD-ROM disc(s). *Sir Speedy, Inc., a nationwide business printer, has equipped more than 300 locations to produce KODAK Photo CD Portfolio discs for customers.*

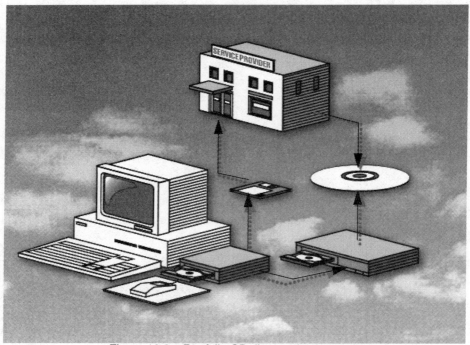

Figure 10.3   Portfolio CD disc production cycle.

KODAK Create-It Photo CD Presentation Software

This section first presents Create-It product description and specifications, followed by a step-by-step tour of this tool in action.

Product Description

KODAK Create-It Photo CD presentation software has all the tools you need to design interactive Photo CD Portfolio presentations. It combines text, graphics image and audio tools into one easy-to-use application for design and layout of Photo CD disc presentations.

You can use Photo CD images and other popular image formats in your presentation, use text tools to create display-text layouts, and edit your material quickly to organize it into multimedia titles with simple drag-and-drop commands.

Create-It lets you make "hot spots" for menu branching and truly interactive presentations. When your presentation is complete you can output color hardcopy or script file. Export a script file from Create-It software to a service center using KODAK Build-It Photo CD Portfolio disc production software to produce a Photo CD Portfolio disc.

System Requirements

- Macintosh II or higher with hard drive
- System 7.0 or higher
- 8- or 24-bit color monitor
- 12 MB of disk space for program storage, dictionary, extensions, templates, and palettes
- 4 MB RAM, 8 MB recommended
- CD-ROM XA drive compatible with the KODAK Photo CD system

Compatibilities

- Import images in Photo CD Master, Pro Photo CD Master, Photo CD Portfolio, TIFF and PICT formats, QuickTime movies.
- Import AIFF audio files (11-, 22, and 44.1-kHz sampling rates).
- Export KODAK Photo CD Portfolio Script Language.
- Export a PICT image of your layout.

Feature Overview

- Create Photo CD Portfolio multimedia presentations using images, text, graphics, and audio.
- Import text, charts, images, and audio popular formats.
- Zoom, rotate, mirror, crop images, and adjust image contrast and color balance, including automated red-eye defect removal.
- Create hot spots for interactive presentations.
- Use spelling checker
- Export KODAK Photo CD Portfolio Script Language for disc creation using Build-It CD Portfolio production software.
- Output color transparencies, slides, or overheads.

Using Create-It Software

The Development Process

As shown in this section, you use Create-It software to produce Photo CD disc presentation, including collateral material such as the CD case insert and labels. The production steps are as follows.

1. Plan your presentation and collateral material. Before you begin:
   a. Ask yourself which medium your portfolio is destined for; Photo-CD disc or paper-output and plan accordingly.
   b. Assemble all the building-block images and audio files.
   c. Talk with your service provider about the preferred method for producing and delivering your presentation for processing.
2. Use separate <u>portfolios</u> to hold separate pieces of the presentation package (for example, one portfolio for the presentation and one portfolio for the CD case insert).
   a. "Portfolio" is KODAK's word for a complete interactive slide presentation.
3. Lay out the frames in each portfolio.
   a. This is the visual creation process where you place images by importing CD photographs, PICT or TIFF picture images, draw graphics, and enter text.
4. Set up the flow of the presentation by assigning menu branch sequences, frame delay times, and audio elements.
   a. By default, Create-It builds a liner presentation that plays each frame for 5 seconds, beginning with the first frame and continuing sequentially through each frame in the portfolio. In this step you can create a customized presentation with branches and menus that give the user choices.
5. Save your portfolios.
6. Preview your Photo CD presentation using the Slide Show command.
7. Print thumbnails of the frames to proof your work.
8. Revise portfolio frames to polish your presentation and any accompanying printed material.
9. Take your portfolios to a service bureau for final Build-It pro-

duction.

10. Assemble your final package.

A Create-It Presentation, Step by Step

We'll walkthrough a typical production sequence that includes adding photo images, text, creating frames, adding branching to the presentation, and finally adding sound.

The Create-It work area has the same familiar look and feel as many other popular multimedia presentation packages, making it easy to get started quickly.

You begin creating your presentation by opening a new portfolio or by opening a template (Fig. 10.4). (Templates designed to get you up and running fast are included with the software.)

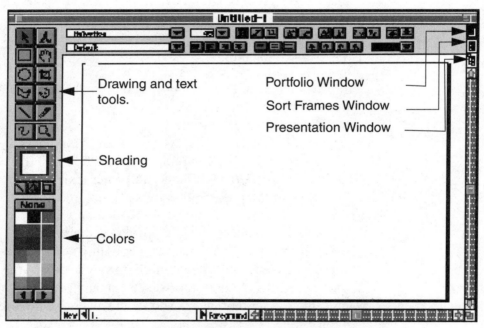

Figure 10.4   Create-It portfolio window.

Adding Photographs and Graphics

To place a photo CD image or graphic on a frame you invoke a read-only graphic or Photo CD palette that displays on the left side of the work space

(Fig. 10.5). CD images from a KODAK Photo disc or graphic file are displayed like a filmstrip in a floating vertical window. Once the photographs or graphic images are displayed, you need only to drag an image onto the work space to place a replica of it on your work space. Once there, you can change its size and add text and other effects to incorporate it into your presentation.

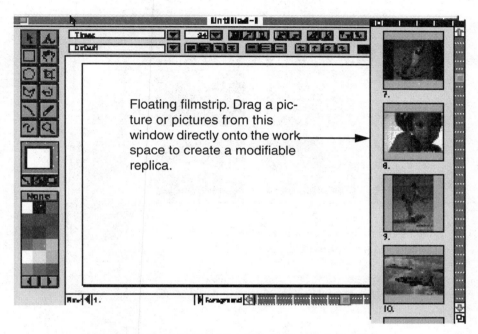

Figure 10.5   A Photo CD palette in the portfolio window.

Text

Once you size and position the imported graphic or photograph in a Portfolio Window, you can add text in any font or size that is installed on your computer. If you use a word processor you'll have no problem with this feature. Once text is entered on the workplace, Create-It treats it like a hybrid graphic-text element. As with any text, you can change fonts, styles, and font size and, as with any graphic object, you can move the text anywhere on the screen even stretch or collapse it to change letterspacing or create custom text.

Working in the Sort Frames Window

A typical presentation is built on full-screen photographs overlaid with text, interactive buttons, and graphics. To create a number of full-screen photographic frames, you work in the Sort Frames window and simply drag photo images onto the work area (Fig. 10.6). You can then quickly reorder and organize each frame simply by placing your cursor on top of it, holding down the mouse button, and dragging it to a new location.

Once you have organized your frames, you can preview the linear presentation using the Slide Show command from the File menu. The frames in your presentation are sequentially shown on screen, from beginning to end.

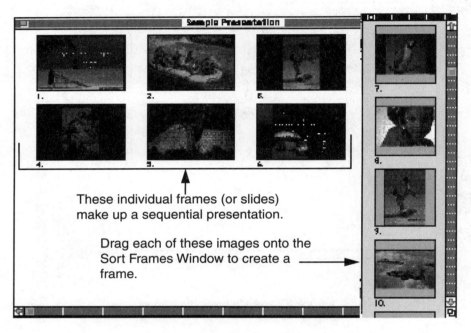

These individual frames (or slides) make up a sequential presentation.

Drag each of these images onto the Sort Frames Window to create a frame.

Figure 10.6   The Sort Frames window.

Creating a Branched Presentation

Branching adds interactive choice to your presentation. You create a branched presentation in the Presentation Window, which allows you to monitor and change a number of related events (Fig. 10.7). The Presentation Window provides a way to see the frames in the current portfolio, determine the viewing order, add audio clips, and create hot spots for branched presentations. The work space is divided into four display areas, and contains a number of elements used to create an interactive presentation as shown in Table 10.1.

TABLE 10.1   Presentation Window Elements

Window Part	Description
Portfolio pane	Displays all the frames in the portfolio
Sequence pane	Displays the viewing order of the frames
Branch pane	Used to define areas of the frame that must be clicked to view branches; these areas are known as *hot spots*
Sound pane	Displays audio files that are available for use with this portfolio
Branch bracket	Holds frames that will be displayed when the corresponding hot spot is clicked
Hotspot indicator	Indicates the number on the Photo CD player remote control that must be pressed, or the area of the frame that must be clicked, to view the branch
Audio icon	Indicates that this frame has audio attached
View icons	Allow you to switch between Edit Frame, Sort Frames, and Presentation views; the top icon symbolizes Edit Frame, the middle icon is for Sort Frames, and the bottom icon is for Presentation view

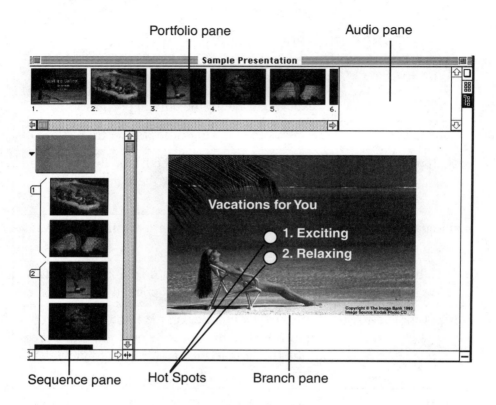

Portfolio pane   Audio pane

Sequence pane   Hot Spots   Branch pane

Figure 10.7   Presentation window.

Adding Audio to the Presentation

Adding audio to a Create-It presentation is a two-step process:

1. You first acquire the audio files using a standard file acquisition dialog box. Once acquired, its name appears in the Audio pane in the Presentation Window.
2. You attach the sound to a frame by placing the cursor on top of the sound's name in the Audio pane, holding down the mouse button, and dragging the sound icon to the branch pane (Fig. 10.8).

Audio file name

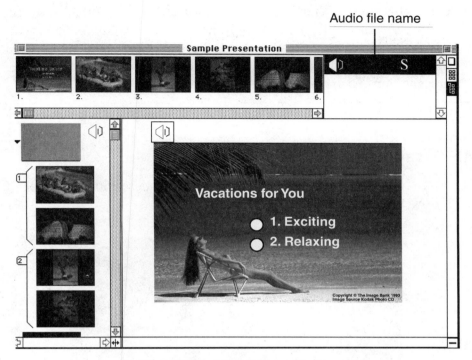

Figure 10.8   Attaching an audio file.

To create a branching presentation, you first drag an image from the sequence pane onto the branch pane, assign hot spots to it, and then assign an action to each hot spot. In Fig. 10.8, when the viewer presses "1. Exciting," the presentation jumps to a river-rafting photo followed by a sequence of other exciting action options. Conversely, if the viewer clicks "Relaxing," the presentation jumps to a series of tranquil vacation scenes.

Once this is done, an audio icon and the sound name are shown at the top-left corner of the menu frame in the branch pane, and to the right of the appropriate frame in the Sequence pane.

Previewing Your Presentation

Create-It lets you view branched and linear presentations to check out your work before sending it on its way for CD production. When you are finished, you can save the presentation and add to it later, or exercise the presentation, just as a user would, by pressing hot spots to navigate through your work.

Create-It Documentation

Create-It comes with an on-line tutorial and Photo CD that show you how to build a typical application. A well-indexed *User's Guide* walks you through the tutorial and describes each of the tool's functions and operations. A flipchart-type handbook, full of tips and hints for creating professional, quality presentations, also comes with the software.

KODAK Arrange-It

This section first presents Arrange-It product description and specifications, followed by a tour of this tool in action.

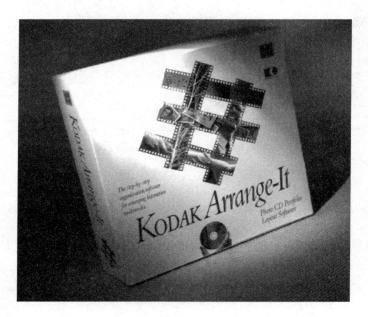

Product Description

KODAK Arrange-It Photo CD Portfolio layout software enables you to systematically lay out sophisticated multimedia presentations in KODAK Photo CD Portfolio format. Arrange-It accepts Create-It frames (and other input) and adds advanced timing, arranging, and other valuable advanced multimedia production capabilities.

Arrange-It lets you create affordable electronic books, training programs, displays, presentations, and other multimedia programs. An intuitive graphical user interface lets you design complex layouts easily, and you can make your presentations interactive using sophisticated multilevel branching.

With Arrange-It, image and audio sequences are seamlessly integrated using its on-screen logical visual layout. When you finish creating your presentation, you export a script file that is used by KODAK Build-It Photo CD Portfolio disc production software to produce a Photo CD Portfolio disc. As with Create-It, you can take the output script to a participating service bureau to have your disc produced.

System Requirements

- Macintosh II or higher with hard drive
- System 7.01 or higher
- 8- or 24-bit color monitor
- 3 MB of disk space for program storage
- 4 MB RAM
- CD ROM XA drive compatible with the KODAK Photo CD system

Compatibilities

- Import images in Photo CD Master, Pro Photo CD Master, Photo CD Portfolio, TIFF and PICT formats.
- Import AIFF audio files (11-, 22-, and 44.1-kHz sampling rates).
- Export KODAK Photo CD Portfolio Script Language.
- Export a PICT image of your layout.

Feature Overview

- Intuitively arrange interactive Photo CD Portfolio multimedia presentations that include images, text, graphics, and audio.
- Use frame design from popular illustrator and image-editing programs, including KODAK Create-It software or KODAK PhotoEdge software, in your Photo CD Portfolio disc layouts.
- Import existing Photo CD Portfolio layouts for a quick start.
- Drag and drop images and audio clips into your layout.

- Control all aspects of Photo CD Portfolio disc structure, including time-out settings, error handling, delays, transitions, and image settings.

- Emulate playback on screen, before your disc is produced.

- KODAK Photo CD Portfolio Script Language for disc creation using Build-It CD Portfolio production software.

Using Arrange-It Software

The Development Process

Arrange-It provides an easy-to-use work space for assembling and arranging complex multimedia presentations. You import images, text, and entire Create-It frames, and arrange them into a cohesive presentation. Before assembling the finished product, you must have all its elements produced and ready to go.

When all the presentation's elements are complete, you import them into Arrange-It and link them to produce a sophisticated interactive presentation.

Arrange-It Tour

Developing a multimedia application using Arrange-It is done in four basic steps:

1. Invoke the Arrange-It software window.
2. Select a collection and add files to it.
3. Create and connect nodes.
4. Play your presentation and check for proper operation.

Using The Arrange-It Software Window

The Arrange-It software window is where you create your presentation, using Photo CD images, PICT and TIFF images, and AIFF audio files from collections. As shown in Fig. 10.9, the Arrange-It window contains the following:

- <u>Collection bar</u>. Displays the collection of images and audio files currently being used. You can display two collection bars at one time to use images from multiple collections when creating your presentation. You can also hide the collection bar(s) to increase the canvas area.

- <u>Ribbon bar</u>. Contains the tools that you use to build your presentation.

- <u>Canvas</u>. The area where files from collections are placed and manipulated for your presentation.

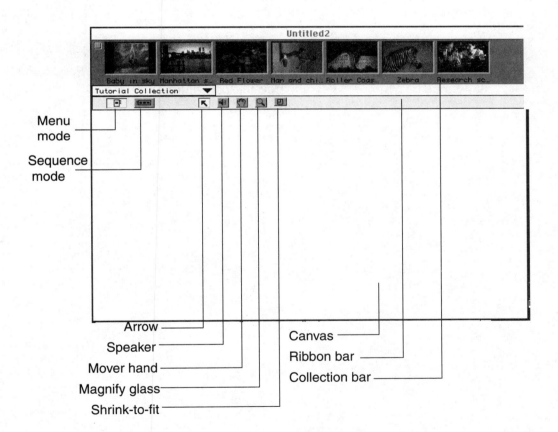

Figure 10.9   The Arrange-It window.

Working with Collections

You can work with collections of slides that you've created using Arrange-It, create a new collection, or add to an existing collection.

You open an existing collection from the tool's collection menu by clicking its name in a file selection dialog box.

Arrange-It lets you import Photo CD images, PICT and TIFF images, and AIF audio files to create new collections or add to existing collections. You can import files that are saved to your hard disk, or you can import files from an external source (for example, from a Photo CD disc, a floppy disk, an optical disk, tape, or a cartridge).

To give you a hands-on feel for Arrange-It, Fig. 10.10 shows how easy it is to add sound and graphics to an existing collection. You first invoke the Edit collections box, and then click Import to display the Import Dialog box.

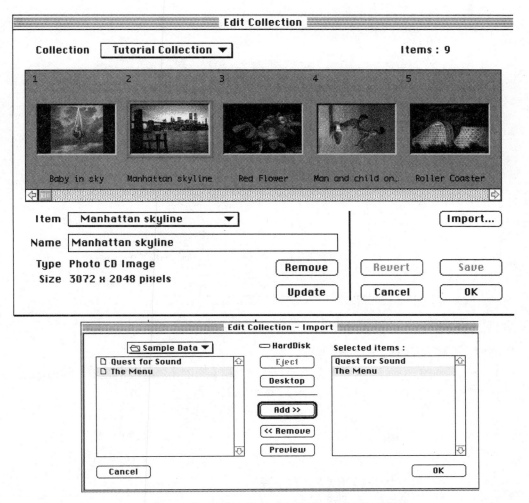

Figure 10.10   Edit collection and Import Dialog boxes.

Add the files to the Import Dialog box's Selected Items scrolling window and press OK to add them to your collection. You can also preview each item before adding it to ensure that it's exactly what you want.

In Fig. 10.11, the Edit Collection window shows the two files (Quest for Sound and the Menu) that were added.

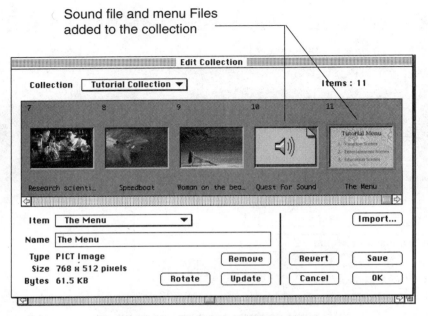

Sound file and menu Files
added to the collection

Figure 10.11   Files added to Edit collection.

Creating and Connecting Nodes

The power of Arrange-It lies in its sophisticated linking capabilities that add true
presentation interactivity, as shown in Fig. 10.12.

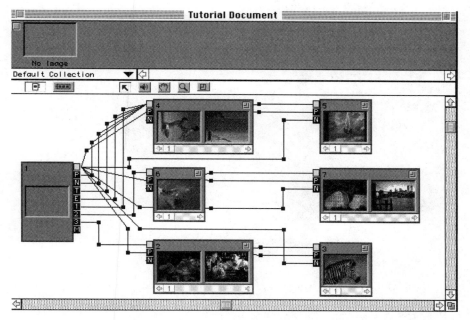

Figure 10.12   Linking nodes for interactivity.

Previewing Your Presentation

As a final step, you use an on-screen virtual remote control unit to see exactly how your presentation will appear once it's distributed on CD disc (Fig. 10.13). When you are finished, you can save the presentation and add to it later, or send the script and associated files to a service bureau that will master a Portfolio CD disc.

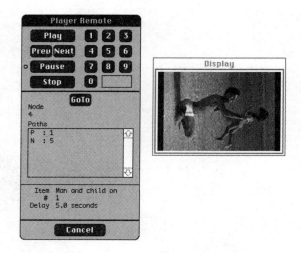

Figure 10.13   Preview the presentation with virtual remote control.

Create-It Documentation

Create-It comes with an on-line tutorial and Photo CD that show you how to build a typical application. A step-by-step tutorial walks you through a typical production cycle, and a *User's Guide* describes each of the tool's functions and operations.

Index